THE MEASUREMENT OF
CUMULATIVE ADVERTISING EFFECTS

1963 Award Winner

THE FORD FOUNDATION DOCTORAL
DISSERTATION SERIES

THE MEASUREMENT OF

CUMULATIVE ADVERTISING EFFECTS

KRISTIAN S. PALDA

Associate Professor
of Marketing
State University of New York
at Buffalo

PRENTICE - HALL, INC.

Englewood Cliffs, N. J.

1960 Award Winners

Bernard H. Baum *Decentralization of Authority in a Bureaucracy*
Dissertation submitted to Department of Sociology, University of Chicago

Leon V. Hirsch *Marketing in an Underdeveloped Economy: The North Indian Sugar Industry*
Dissertation submitted to Graduate School of Business Administration, Harvard University

Bedros Peter Pashigian *The Distribution of Automobiles, an Economic Analysis of the Franchise System*
Dissertation submitted to Department of Economics, Massachusetts Institute of Technology

Martin Patchen *The Choice of Wage Comparison*
Dissertation submitted to Department of Social Psychology, University of Michigan

Fred M. Tonge *A Heuristic Program for Assembly Line Balancing*
Dissertation submitted to Graduate School of Industrial Administration, Carnegie Institute of Technology

1959 Award Winners

Kalman J. Cohen *Computer Models of the Shoe, Leather, Hide Sequence*
Dissertation submitted to Graduate School of Industrial Administration, Carnegie Institute of Technology

Bob R. Holdren *The Structure of a Retail Market and the Market Behavior of Retail Units*
Dissertation submitted to Department of Economics, Yale University

Frank Proschan *Polya Type Distributions in Renewal Theory, with an Application to an Inventory Problem*
Dissertation submitted to Department of Statistics, Stanford University

Andrew C. Stedry *Budget Control and Cost Behavior*
Dissertation submitted to Graduate School of Industrial Administration, Carnegie Institute of Technology

Victor H. Vroom *Some Personality Determinants of the Effects of Participation*
Dissertation submitted to Department of Psychology, University of Michigan

1962 Award Winners

Alexander Barges *The Effect of Capital Structure on the Cost of Capital*
Dissertation submitted to Graduate School of Business Administration, Northwestern University

Chalres P. Bonini *Simulation of Information and Decision Systems in the Firm*
Dissertation submitted to Graduate School of Business, Carnegie Institute of Technology

James M. Ferguson *The Advertising Rate Structure in the Daily Newspaper Industry*
Dissertation submitted to Department of Economics, University of Chicago

Gordon M. Kaufman *Statistical Decision and Related Techniques in Oil and Gas Exploration*
Dissertation submitted to Graduate School of Business, Harvard University

H. Martin Weingartner *Mathematical Programming and the Analysis of Capital Budgeting Problems*
Dissertation submitted to Graduate School of Industrial Administration Carnegie Institute of Technology

1961 Award Winners

Geoffrey P. E. Clarkson *Portfolio Selection: A Simulation of Trust Investment*
Dissertation submitted to Graduate School of Industrial Administration, Carnegie Institute of Technology

Donald E. Farrar *The Investment Decision Under Uncertainty: Portfolio Selection*
Dissertation submitted to Faculty of Arts and Sciences, Harvard University

Richard S. Hatch *An Evaluation of a Forced-Choice Differential Accuracy Approach to the Measurement of Supervisory Empathy*
Dissertation submitted to Department of Psychology, University of Minnesota

David Meiselman *The Term Structure of Interest Rates*
Dissertation submitted to Department of Economics, University of Chicago

George William Summers *Financing and Initial Operations of New Firms*
Dissertation submitted to Department of Management, Case Institute of Technology

A Isabel et Kristian Filip

Foreword

Dr. Palda's dissertation, completed during the academic year 1962–1963, is one of six selected for publication in the fifth annual Doctoral Dissertation Competition sponsored by the Program in Economic Development and Administration of the Ford Foundation.

The intent of the doctoral dissertation competition has been to recognize and encourage excellence in research on business by graduate students. Publication awards, now totaling twenty-six, have been made over the five years of the competition to persons granted doctorates in business and related fields whose thesis research on problems of business was especially distinguished by its analytical content and strong roots in the underlying disciplines common to business.

In addition to Dr. Palda's, the dissertations published this year are:

The Demand for Liquid Assets: A Temporal Cross-Section Analysis
> Edgar Louis Feige
> Department of Economics
> University of Chicago

An Evaluation of Level of Aspiration As a Training Procedure
> Forrest W. Fryer
> Department of Psychology
> University of Maryland

The Demand for Physical Capital: Application of a Wealth Model
> Frederick S. Hammer
> Graduate School of Industrial Administration
> Carnegie Institute of Technology

Some Large Scale-Production Scheduling Problems in the Paper Industry
> John F. Pierce, Jr.
> School of Industrial Management
> Massachusetts Institute of Technology

*The Economics of Discretionary Behavior: Managerial Objectives in a
Theory of the Firm*
        Oliver E. Williamson
        Graduate School of Industrial Administration
        Carnegie Institute of Technology

On behalf of the Ford Foundation, I wish to express my gratitude to
the members of the Editorial Committee for the care and thought they
devoted to the selection process. The members of this Committee,
who made the final selection of winning dissertations, were: Professor
Robert Ferber of the University of Illinois, Professor Mason Haire of
the University of California at Berkeley, and Professor Thomas L.
Whisler of the University of Chicago.

The Editorial Committee's task was considerably lightened by the
assistance of twelve readers, experts in the wide range of disciplines
covered in the competition, who carefully screened the theses submitted. The Foundation joins the Committee in acknowledging their
debt to Professors Paul E. Breer of Cornell University, Earl F. Cheit
and Lyman W. Porter of the University of California at Berkeley,
James R. Jackson of the University of California at Los Angeles, Arch
R. Dooley of Harvard University, Daniel M. Holland of the Massachusetts Institute of Technology, Robert J. Holloway of the University
of Minnesota, Donald P. Jacobs of Northwestern University, Bernard
Karsh of the University of Illinois, Walter G. Kell of the University
of Michigan, E. W. Martin, Jr. of Indiana University, and Joseph W.
Newman of Stanford University.

With the publication of these latest winners, the Doctoral Dissertation Competition has completed its planned five-year span. My col-
leagues and I wish to express our appreciation for the generous assistance
which the Ford Foundation has received from many people: Faculty
members too numerous to mention have read and screened the more
than 250 dissertations which have been submitted during the life of the
competition, and Prentice-Hall has contributed its services to the
publicizing and publishing of the selected dissertations.

                                    CLARENCE H. FAUST
                                    VICE PRESIDENT
                                    THE FORD FOUNDATION

New York, N.Y.
January, 1964

Preface

Stigler said that the most interesting aspect of advertising is its cumulative effect—the fact that the effects of advertising persist beyond the period of expenditure and become a valuable if intangible asset of the company.[1]

It is the objective of this dissertation to determine whether the measurement of cumulative advertising effects can be attempted or improved by having recourse to the model of distributed lags proposed by Koyck. A corollary objective is to ascertain in a particular instance—that of the Lydia E. Pinkham Medicine Company—the existence, importance and measurability of long-run effects of advertising.

The computational work connected with this thesis deserves mention. Briefly, limited access to computer facilities made it necessary to estimate most of the regressions in one batch. (This was done on the University of Chicago's Univac I computer.) Past results could not, therefore, be used to any appreciable extent in the setting up of more "promising" model versions. The exception to this are a few "second-generation" estimates which were calculated on the IBM 1620 computer of the Ecole des Hautes Etudes Commerciales de l'Universite de Montreal.

The impetus to study the effects of advertising came from the chairman of my dissertation committee, Professor Lester G. Telser, whose vigorous advice was received gratefully throughout the course of this study. Professor Harry V. Roberts, never satisfied and always helpful, unmercifully raised my standard of performance. Professor John E. Jeuck generously put his deep knowledge of business at my disposal and combatted inelegance of thought and expression in successive versions of this thesis. Needless to say, I alone am responsible for the shortcomings that remain. I also benefited from the help of Professor George J. Stigler and the financial assistance of the Charles R. Walgreen Foundation. A part of the research work for this dissertation was accomplished while I held a University (of Chicago) Fellowship.

---

[1] George J. Stigler, *The Theory of Price* (New York: The Macmillan Company, 1952), p. 208.

I am indebted to Messrs. Arthur Pinkham, president, and Hermon E. Smith, vice-president of the Lydia E. Pinkham Medicine Company who made this study possible by giving me access to the records of the company and by answering all my questions. Mr. Charles Pinkham, the former advertising manager of the company, gave me some valuable information.

Mr. Jeff Schmaltz was responsible for the Univac calculations at the University of Chicago while Professor Claude Tricot of the Ecole des Hautes Etudes Commerciales (de Montreal) helped with the computation of the "second-generation" estimates.

KRISTIAN S. PALDA

Contents

Contents

THE MEASUREMENT OF
CUMULATIVE ADVERTISING EFFECTS

CHAPTER 1

On the Measurement of
Advertising Effectiveness

Even though advertising has assumed a large part in the selling efforts of consumer goods industries, progress in the measurement of its effectiveness has been slow. Thus, while it is often considered to be an important factor in the stimulation of demand, the individual firm finds it difficult to determine the size of its advertising budget with reasonable confidence. In 1951 the total volume of advertising in this country was estimated at $6.5 billion. Eleven years later, when this figure had doubled, the situation then described by Joel Dean had not substantially changed:

> Primary attention has been given to the problem of how to get the most out of a given advertising expenditure. Determining the size of that expenditure from its effectiveness has been relatively neglected. The amount of money spent on advertising and the lack of defensible objective criteria for determining how much to spend argue cogently for more research on the problem of budgeting.[1]

This unsatisfactory state of affairs can largely be traced to the difficulty of isolating the influence of advertising from the welter of other factors that also bear on sales. It is this difficulty that probably accounts for the fact that most published empirical studies confine

---

[1] Joel Dean, *Managerial Economics* (Englewood Cliffs, N.J.: Prentice-Hall, Inc., 1951), p. 385.

their attention to problems dealing with the optimum allocation of a given advertising budget. Investigations of that type deal frequently with fairly straightforward relationships (or so it would seem) between two variables. Also they usually dispense with sales as the criterion of effectiveness. The following quotation from a recent publication dealing with the appraisal of advertising effects illustrates a fairly prevalent attitude among advertisers:

> Generally, it is not considered reasonable to use sales results as a basis of measuring advertising effectiveness, except where advertising is the dominant sales force, where other factors affecting sales remain fairly constant, and where the results of the advertising are quickly reflected in shipments and billings. Where these conditions do not exist, other yardsticks must usually be used.[1]

So restrictive a position may be due, in part, to the advertisers' unfamiliarity with modern methods of multivariate analysis. However, anyone who concerns himself with the evaluation of advertising performance will at least sympathize with it. In situations in which there are frequent changes in the marketing mix of the brand, how can fluctuations in its sales be easily ascribed to a changing advertising appropriation? Or, indeed, how can the effect of a change in the advertising mix itself be evaluated in terms of sales?

The difficulties being patently obvious, a piecemeal way of measurement is very often resorted to. For example, the relative efficacy of different headline positions may be, as a first step, appraised in terms of reader attention. As the next step, several versions of copy may be pre-tested, using audience preferences as a criterion. Further steps may include a judicial evaluation of the particular media vehicle to be selected, employing circulation figures as a yardstick. With the help of such a step-by-step procedure the advertiser attempts to polish each component of his advertising effort to perfection. It is a widely held opinion that such a process will lead to a total advertising effort which will be the best that can be achieved under the circumstances.[2]

---

[1] H. D. Wolfe, G. K. Brown and G. C. Thompson, *Measuring Advertising Results* (New York: National Industrial Conference Board, 1962, Business Policy Study No. 102), p. 7.

[2] Lester R. Frankel in Russell H. Colley (ed.), *Evaluating Advertising Effectiveness.* Vol. VII of *Practical Guides and Modern Practices for Better Advertising Management* (New York: Association of National Advertisers, 1959), p. 336.

Another opinion encountered in advertising circles relates to what might be called a hierarchical sequence of effects.[1] A version of it holds that, typically, when a message is perceived, it is first evaluated in such simple terms as like or dislike. Then, on a "higher" plane, information may be acquired and retained. In turn, this may lead to the formation of an attitude toward the subject-matter of the message. If the attitude persists long enough it may induce overt behavior.

The combined effect of these two opinions inclines advertisers toward what might be called "limited objective" research. A single ingredient of the advertising effort is selected for scrutiny and evaluated in terms of an effect deemed not too "distant" from it. Then another advertising ingredient would be judged by effects seemingly easy to link up with it, and so on. This procedure, it is thought, avoids the unpleasant problem of "intervening variables" which appears when sales are linked directly to advertising expenditure. Starch readership studies are perhaps the most typical illustration of "limited objective" research in advertising. In the terminology of mass communications, such studies appraise message content and form (copy, art and layout) in terms of information acquired (recall).

Two assumptions are at work in such research procedures. The first is that the effects of copy can be considered in isolation from the other parts of the advertising effort. The second is that the stage at which effect is measured is part of a unidirectional flow of causation whose culminating point is purchase.

The whole tenor of mass communications findings makes it clear that the independent variables in the communications process are inter-related with respect to the final effects (such as attitude formation or overt behavior).[2] This renders the first assumption tenuous. The second assumption has stubbornly resisted satisfactory verification (at least in the advertising field), despite repeated attempts and claims of success.[3] Indeed, Cox, in a lengthy interpretation of mass communications find-

---

[1] It is related to certain somewhat imprecisely formulated tenets of social psychology. A recent article develops a hierarchical sequence of effects similar to the one mentioned in the text. See Harold Mendelsohn, "Measuring the Process of Communications Effect," *Public Opinion Quarterly*, **XXVI** (Fall, 1962), 411–16.

[2] Joseph T. Klapper, *The Effects of Mass Communications* (New York: The Free Press of Glencoe, Inc., 1960).

[3] "Dr. Daniel Starch's New Study—Measuring Product Sales Made by Advertising," *Printer's Ink*, February 16, 1962.

ings in terms of their significance to advertising, makes the following statement:

1. It is possible for a person to change his factual knowledge without changing his attitudes or his behavior.
2. It is possible for a person to change his behavior without first changing his attitudes (i.e., attitude change may follow behavior change).[1]

"Limited objective" research was considered from the point of view of social psychology. From the standpoint of managerial economics, the step-by-step measurement procedure can be regarded as forming a part of the sub-optimization process which aims at maximum productivity of each advertising input. However, the quest for maximum effectiveness of each advertising ingredient does not necessarily spell the greatest over-all effectiveness of the total advertising effort. Also, it is difficult to compare the costs of marginal physical products of the various advertising inputs, as these are expressed in different units of measurement (circulation figures, opinion ratings, etc.). As Howard puts it: "A shortcoming of much advertising research is the failure to relate the conclusions of effectiveness to costs so that meaningful alternatives can be presented to management."[2]

These reflections lead to the conviction that while "limited objective" research is often necessary, it is not in itself sufficient for management's purposes.[3] It should be complemented by "total effect" research which measures the relationship of advertising outlay to sales directly.

If, for instance, a firm tries to measure the influence of the selection of a particular medium upon sales, it confines itself to the estimation of the marginal revenue product of one advertising input. This is a task it must undertake if it wants to attain a least-cost combination of the resources that go into its advertising production function. However, no matter how useful such an estimate would be, it cannot answer the question of how much a firm should spend on advertising. Moreover, if the firm is to maximize the present value of its net receipts, it must

---

[1] Donald F. Cox, "Clues for Advertising Strategists," *Harvard Business Review*, Vol. **XXXIX** (November–December, 1961), sixth and seventh page in reprint with unnumbered pages.

[2] John A. Howard, *Marketing Management* (Homewood, Ill.: Richard D. Irwin, Inc., 1957), p. 327.

[3] "Limited objective" research clearly finds its most useful field of application in the preparation and diffusion of advertisements—a task typically performed by advertising *agencies* and not *advertisers*.

allocate its budget among competing ends such as plant, equipment, inventories, research and advertising in such a way as to equate the marginal rate of return on capital with the marginal cost of it. This— clearly a top management responsibility—definitely requires the estimation (albeit often informal) of the shape of the total advertising production function. Frequently such estimation will have to be made in a multi-period, dynamic context.[1]

The several arguments in support of the "total effect" approach in research dealing with the measurement of advertising effects can be supplemented by an additional one of a less formal, but highly practical nature. The growing employment of concepts and measurement methods of the behavioral sciences in "limited objective" research has very likely improved its quality. Without doubt the improved quality was bought at considerably increased cost. Therefore, incentives are not lacking to tread a different path.

A survey of a few pertinent scholarly journals indicates that the path suggested here has not, as yet, been frequently trodden. The *Journal of Marketing*, since its appearance in 1936, has carried three articles reporting on empirical research into the link between *total* advertising effort and sales. Wagner's article enquired into the effects of industry-wide advertising (cigarettes, autos, department stores) on sales against the background of a business cycle.[2] Berreman looked at the (simple) correlation between indices of advertising expenditure and sales of individual (unnamed) novels. His efforts to uncover a relationship between the two were not very successful.[3] Dickins reported a simple before-and-after experiment in which it was found that the use of advertising posters stimulated the sale of milk.[4]

Since its inception in 1928 *The Journal of Business of the University of Chicago* has carried more reports on the measurement of total advertising effect in terms of sales than any other scholarly periodical. In 1931 Cover *et al.* made a graphic analysis of the relationship between fluctuations in sales of department stores and the lineage of their newspaper advertising (taken as the best available indicator of advertising

---

[1] Marc Nerlove and Kenneth J. Arrow, "Optical Advertising Policy Under Dynamic Conditions," *Economica*, **XXXIX** (May, 1962), 129–42.

[2] Louis C. Wagner, "Advertising and the Business Cycle," *Journal of Marketing*, **VI** (October, 1941), 124–35.

[3] Joel V. Berreman, "Advertising and the Sale of Novels," *Journal of Marketing*, **VII** (January, 1943), 234–41.

[4] Dorothy Dickins, "Advertising Dairy Products in Rural Grocery Stores," *Journal of Marketing*, **XIX** (January, 1955), 268–70.

outlays).[1] A pioneering study of the demand for cigarettes appeared two years later. In it, per capita yearly consumption of cigarettes was regressed on "real" price of a thousand cigarettes, on the amounts spent by the leading four cigarette companies on newspaper advertising, and on time. Though the author, Schoenberg, was primarily interested in the price-quantity relationship, he carefully analyzed advertising's influence as well.[2] Cowan contributed an ingenious cross-sectional study of the relation between regional circulation figures of the *Saturday Evening Post* (which carried Chevrolet advertisements) and regional Chevrolet registrations. The method used was cross-tabulation and yielded, among other things, data suitable for marginal analysis.[3] Brown and Mancina tested the hypothesis that the relationship between the sales and advertising expenditures of 108 department stores could be expressed by a linear function. Analysis of (residual) variance did not yield conclusive results.[4] In 1947 Roberts wrote an article which remains a classic in the field of advertising measurement. Using multiple regression techniques, he analyzed consumer panel data on two rival brands of a pharmaceutical product. He succeeded, among other things, in isolating the net influence of A's advertising on B's sales.[5] In 1955 Tull examined the decline of sales of Sapolio soap and reached the conclusion that advertising outlays were not to blame. He did not employ statistical techniques.[6]

Since 1922, when it first started publication, the *Harvard Business Review* carried two articles about the appraisal of total advertising effort by the criterion of sales. In 1927 Vaile published a study dealing with the variations in advertising lineage and sales of more than two hundred companies during one business cycle (1920–1924).[7] In a 1949

---

[1] J. H. Cover *et al.*, "Department Stores Sales and Advertising," *The Journal of Business of the University of Chicago*, **IV** (July, 1931), 227–44.

[2] E. H. Schoenberg, "The Demand Curve for Cigarettes," *Journal of Business*, **VI** (January, 1933), 15–31. The period analyzed was 1923 to 1931.

[3] Donald R. G. Cowan, "Sales Analysis from the Management Standpoint," *Journal of Business*, **IX** (July, 1936), 170–88.

[4] George H. Brown and Frank A. Mancina, "A Note on the Relationship Between Sales and Advertising of Department Stores," *Journal of Business*, **XIII** (January, 1940), 1–16, and correction appearing on p. 205 of the same volume.

[5] Harry V. Roberts, "The Measurement of Advertising Results," *Journal of Business*, **XX** (July, 1947), 131–45.

[6] Donald S. Tull, "A Re-examination of the Causes of the Decline in Sales of Sapolio," *Journal of Business*, **XXVIII** (April, 1955), 128–37.

[7] Roland S. Vaile, "Use of Advertising During Depressions," *Harvard Business Review*, **V** (April, 1927), 323–30.

article, Hollander wrote about the investigation of the influence of advertising on the sales of a nationally distributed (anonymous) drug product. His description of the graphic multiple correlation analysis he used is not sufficiently clear, but he claimed to have been able to determine the value of the cumulative advertising effect.[1]

Operations Research, one of the newer journals in fields which may be expected to be interested in the advertising evaluation problem, published in 1957 an article which quickly received wide attention. The authors claim to have discovered patterns of sales response to advertising outlays that are susceptible to generalizations. Controlled advertising experiments conducted by major industrial concerns with a number of products (names undisclosed) have apparently revealed the existence of certain parameters such as the Sales Decay Constant, which gives the rate at which customers are lost when advertising is stopped. The reader is not offered enough information to permit verification.[2] *Applied Statistics* and the *Journal of Industrial Economics* published no articles on the subject.

The *Journal of Farm Economics* (checked from 1930 on) published in 1961 a noteworthy study of the effects of advertising, using an ingenious econometric approach.[3]

Thus it appears that most of the efforts to relate sales to advertising are more than a decade old. Relatively little attention to this subject is found even in the pages of the publication most closely identified with advertising research, the *Journal of Advertising Research*. A recently launched (September, 1960) quarterly, it carries in its first five issues one article devoted to an empirical study (by multiple regression methods) of cross-sectional advertising outlay and sales data[4] and one in which the net influence of advertising outlays on sales was incidentally touched upon.[5]

---

[1] Sidney Hollander, "A Rationale for Advertising Expenditures," *Harvard Business Review*, **XXVII** (January, 1949), 79–87.

[2] M. L. Vidale and H. B. Wolfe, "An Operations-Research Study of Sales Response to Advertising," *Operations Research*, **V** (June, 1957), 370–81.

[3] Marc Nerlove and Frederick V. Waugh, "Advertising Without Supply Control: Some Implications of a Study of the Advertising of Oranges," *Journal of Farm Economics*, **XLIII** (October, 1961), 813–37.

[4] Frank Meissner, "Sales and Advertising of Lettuce," *Journal of Advertising Research*, **I** (March, 1961), 1–10.

[5] Seymour Banks, "Some Correlates of Coffee and Cleanser Brand Shares," *Journal of Advertising Research*, **I** (June, 1961), 22–28.

Research into "total" advertising effectiveness can be conveniently classed into two categories. Experimental investigations and cross-sectional analysis deal typically with the measurement of variables over a single period of time, while the analysis of time series stretches over several time periods. Experiments, varying from the simplest "before-and-after without control group" sales test to more elaborate designs may quite possibly be the method most frequently employed by advertisers. The previously mentioned study undertaken by the National Industrial Conference Board reports in a very laconic manner on 92 case studies of advertising effectiveness.[1] Of the 18 which related sales to advertising expenditures, 13 used the experimental approach, 2 analyzed cross-sectional data and 3 looked at data generated over time. Despite their apparent frequency, controlled advertising experiments are scantily reported in learned journals, possibly because of the commercial secrecy surrounding them. Typically, the cost of experimentation or the absence of regional breakdowns leads to the consideration of sales, advertising and other data generated over time. Since such data can sometimes be found in published sources, independent researchers get a chance to study advertising effects, often from a welfare standpoint.[2]

However useful they may be, market tests and cross-sectional studies may not always yield adequate results. Briefly, they usually cannot take account of the cumulative effects of advertising.

From this point on, attention will be restricted to advertising that may reasonably be presumed to have some cumulative effect over time. Sometimes it is called "franchise building" and it is chiefly engaged in by manufacturers of nationally advertised brands of consumer goods.[3] Cumulative or lagged effects of advertising may be defined as: (1) the effects of a perceived advertisement which influences two or more successive purchasing decisions of a consumer with regard to a given product (or brand of a product), or (2) the effects of an advertisement which influences consumer buying behavior beyond the period of its appearance.

---

[1] Wolfe, Brown and Thompson, *op. cit.*

[2] An example is Richard B. Tennant, *The American Cigarette Industry* (New Haven, Conn.: Yale University Press, 1950), pp. 163–72.

[3] A comprehensive definition is given in C. E. Eldridge, "Advertising Effectiveness—How Can It Be Measured?" *Journal of Marketing*, **XXII** (January, 1958), 241–51.

Some reasons that may account for the existence of a time lag between the appearance of an advertising message and the final increment of sales stimulated thereby are:

1. Continued brand preference, though probably maintained by satisfaction with the quality of the product, may have its origin in the action of a single, long-forgotten ad.
2. It may take a series of ads to break through a threshold of buying resistance. The last ad which triggers the purchase cannot alone be credited with the result.
3. The potential customer, persuaded though he may be by the ad, is not immediately in the market for the product.
4. A particularly lengthy lag may result when a product can only be used from a certain age on. A "persuaded" parent may have to wait for some time before imparting his preference to offspring.

The idea that the effect of much advertising is spread over time is by no means new: indeed, since a long-term phenomenon is presumably more difficult to appraise than a short-term one, it has probably discouraged attempts to measure "total" advertising effectiveness.

A theoretical article by Jastram explored many of the implications of cumulative advertising effects for the policy of the firm. It also gave additional reasons for the existence of lagged effects: "indirect action" copy aimed primarily at building up brand associations that would only ultimately lead to purchase (institutional advertising being an extreme example), "durable" media, such as magazines, which are read months after their date of publication and a long distributive channel used by the advertiser, causing retail sales fluctuations to appear at factory level only months later.[1] This last factor would not be covered by the previously offered definition of a lagged effect and is not considered by the writer as causing a "true" advertising lag. Jastram also gives references to other articles that have acknowledged in some significant manner the existence of delayed advertising effects. Let it also be mentioned that Borden, reporting on his massive investigation of the economic effects of advertising, makes repeated reference to the existence of lagged advertising effects.[2]

---

[1] Roy W. Jastram, "A Treatment of Distributed Lags in the Theory of Advertising Expenditure," *Journal of Marketing*, XX (July, 1955), 36–46.

[2] Neil H. Borden, *The Economic Effects of Advertising* (Homewood, Ill.: Richard D. Irwin, Inc., 1952), pp. 104, 105, 135, 137, 140.

The most recent articles that come to grips with the problem of lingering advertising effects in a theoretical vein are by Arrow and Nerlove,[1] Kuehn[2] and Jessen.[3] The last proposes an experimental design that would be able to measure delayed effects.

The writer is aware of only four attempts at empirical ascertainment or measurement of cumulative advertising effect. Hollander[4] and the team of Vidale and Wolfe[5] claim they have detected it, but their assertions cannot be verified without access to data that were not published by the authors. Tull has discovered the existence of a lag in a study of Packer's Tar Soap but has not measured it.[6] Only Nerlove and Waugh have measured it and they so fully reported on it that their work can be re-checked by others.[7]

If it is true that delayed effects are the rule rather than the exception in national consumer goods advertising, it becomes clear that data captured over a brief period of time could furnish incomplete evidence from which to judge the productivity of advertising dollars. Data collected from controlled experiments or for purposes of cross-sectional analysis are rarely gathered over a period of more than a few months. In the previously mentioned cross-sectional study of consumer panel data (which were generated over a six-months period) Roberts makes this remark: "The most serious assumption is that the advertising-sales relationship derived is said to reflect only the advertising of the particular time period studied . . . this represents the most important qualification to the remaining conclusions of this study."[8]

It does not follow that a lag, if it exists, will automatically be disclosed when time series is subjected to regression analysis. Particular regression models that may do so are considered next.

---

[1] *Loc. cit.*

[2] Alfred A. Kuehn, "How Advertising Performance Depends on Other Marketing Factors," *Journal of Advertising Research*, **II** (March, 1962), 2–10.

[3] R. J. Jessen, "A Switch—Over Experimental Design to Measure Advertising Effect," *Journal of Advertising Research*, **I** (March, 1961), 11–24.

[4] *Loc. cit.*

[5] *Loc. cit.*

[6] Donald S. Tull, "An Examination of the Hypothesis that Advertising Has a Lagged Effect on Sales" (unpublished Ph.D. dissertation, University of Chicago, 1956).

[7] *Loc. cit.*

[8] *Loc. cit.*, p. 138.

Distributed Lags

The term *distributed lags* is used to describe a phenomenon in which a stimulus evokes a full reaction only after some passage of time, after some lag. The total effect is not felt in the same period that the cause occurred but is distributed over time.

The concept of distributed lags was first used and discussed by Irving Fisher in 1925.[1] Algebraically, the effect of an independent variable x (for example, monthly advertising outlays) which affects a dependent variable y (for example, sales) over time may be expressed in the following manner:

$$(2.1) \qquad y_t = f(x_t, x_{t-1}, x_{t-2}, \ldots)$$

The problem is to determine what form the distribution of the lag assumes. In 1937 Fisher suggested a criterion by which this determination ought to be judged and proposed a method to do it.[2] However, it was not until Koyck published a monograph on the subject nearly twenty years later that the use of distributed lags became widespread in work of econometric nature.[3] Such work ranges from studies of monetary phenomena to analyses of demand and has been surveyed (up to 1958) by Nerlove.[4]

---

[1] Irving Fisher, "Our Unstable Dollar and the So-Called Business Cycle," *Journal of the American Statistical Association*, **XX** (1925), 179–202.

[2] Irving Fisher, "Note on a Short-Cut Method for Calculating Distributed Lags," *Bulletin de l'Institut International de la Statistique*, **XXIX** (1937), 323–27.

[3] L. M. Koyck, *Distributed Lags and Investment Analysis* (Amsterdam: North-Holland Publishing Co., 1954).

[4] Marc Nerlove, *Distributed Lags and Demand Analysis for Agricultural and Other Commodities*, U.S. Department of Agriculture Handbook No. 141 (Washington, D.C.: Government Printing Office, June, 1958).

Equation (2.1) can be written as a linear approximation:

(2.2) $y_t = \alpha_0 x_t + \alpha_1 x_{t-1} + \alpha_2 x_{t-2} + \cdots$

If no further assumption is made about the form of the distribution of the lag, it may be desirable to estimate the coefficients by multiple regression. In cases where a lag is suspected to be present, this procedure may be superior to regressions that relate the independent to the dependent variable at concurrent points of time only.

However, one question is in knowing when to stop adding lagged independent variables to the estimating equation. Alt thought that a stop should be called when the coefficients of the additional independent variables cease making economic sense or when their standard error becomes too large.[1]

Fisher was willing to assume that the influence of x on y is greatest at the very next time unit and then tapers off by equal decrements for each successive time unit. This would mean that the distribution curve of the lags approximates a straight line, beginning one time unit after the cause. A specific illustration of an estimating equation would be:

(2.3) $$y_t = a + b\,\frac{(3x_t + 2x_{t-1} + x_{t-2})}{6}$$

Several other equations expressing various patterns of lag would be estimated. The one yielding the highest correlation would be chosen as best representing the distribution of the lag.[2]

An ingenious method of side-stepping this trial-and-error process has been devised by Koyck.[3] It will be described briefly and applied to the advertising-sales situation.

Assume that S_t, the firm's sales revenue at time t, is a linear function of its own past and present advertising outlays, A_i, only. This can be expressed in stochastic form as

(2.4) $S_t = a + \alpha_0 A_t + \alpha_1 A_{t-1} + \cdots + u_t$

where u_t is a random disturbance.[4]

A further simplifying step is to suppose that the series of coefficients

---

[1] F. L. Alt, "Distributed Lags," *Econometrica*, **X** (April, 1942), 113–28.

[2] Fisher, *loc. cit.*

[3] Koyck, *op. cit.*, pp. 19–39.

[4] It is reasonable to assume that the α's are not so small as to bring a swift disappearance of sales, nor so large as to lead to an increase without limit in the firm's advertising appropriation.

$\alpha_i (i = 0, 1, 2, \cdots)$, from a certain index $i = k$, can be approximated by a convergent geometric series:

$$(2.5) \qquad \alpha_{k+m} = \lambda \alpha_{k+m-1}$$

where $m \geqslant 0$ and $0 < \lambda < 1$. From such a hypothesis it follows that

$$(2.6) \qquad S_t = a + \alpha_0 A_t + \alpha_1 A_{t-1} + \cdots + \alpha_{k-1} A_{t-k-1} + \alpha_k A_{t-k}$$

$$+ \alpha_k \lambda A_{t-k-1} + \alpha_k \lambda^2 A_{t-k-2} + \cdots + u_t, \quad \text{when} \quad K \geqslant 0$$

Thus sales revenue is a function of $k - 1$ unweighted lagged advertising outlays and a geometrically weighted average of all other past advertising expenditures. Figure 1 gives a graphic representation of the time-shape of such a reaction of sales to advertising when $k = 2$, $\alpha_0 = .5$, $\alpha_1 = 1$ and $\lambda = .5$.

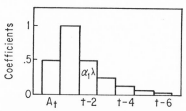

Fig. 1. Time-shape of reaction of sales to advertising

If the reaction of the dependent variable is taken to assume the distribution of a geometric progression from the very first period on (when $k = 0$), the simpler expression (2.7) is obtained:

$$(2.7) \qquad S_t = a + \alpha A_t + \alpha \lambda A_{t-1} + \alpha \lambda^2 A_{t-2} + \cdots + u_t$$

Now lag (2.7) one period, multiply it by λ and subtract the resulting (2.8) from (2.7):

$$(2.7) \qquad S_t = a + \alpha A_t + \alpha \lambda A_{t-1} + \alpha \lambda^2 A_{t-2} + \cdots + u_t$$

$$(2.8) \qquad \lambda S_{t-1} = \lambda a + \alpha \lambda A_{t-1} + \alpha \lambda^2 A_{t-2} + \cdots + u_{t-1}$$

$$(2.9) \qquad S_t = (1 - \lambda)a + \alpha A_t + \lambda S_{t-1} + u_t - \lambda u_{t-1}$$

Equation (2.9) merits consideration. Least squares estimates of its parameters will have the large-sample, asymptotic properties of consistency and efficiency under the four usual assumptions.[1] These are:

[1] "If the estimate α^* converges in probability to α as n tends to infinity, α^* is a consistent estimate of α." Harald Cramér, *Mathematical Methods of Statistics* (Princeton: Princeton University Press, 1946), p 489.

"The statistic f is an efficient estimate of theta if, as the sample size increases toward infinity, the distribution of f tends toward the normal distribution with mean theta, and variance less than that of any other statistic which is also asymptotically normally distributed with mean theta . . .. The efficiency criterion applies only in the limit as n approaches infinity, while the condition for best unbiasedness holds for all size samples." Lawrence R. Klein, *A Textbook of Econometrics* (New York: Harper & Row, Publishers, 1953), p. 53.

(1) u_t, for every t, has zero expected value, (2) the variance of u_t is constant over time, (3) the disturbance term, u_t, is not correlated with any predetermined variable, (4) the disturbance terms of different time periods are linearly independent.

Should there be correlation between an independent variable and the disturbance, the least squares estimates would be biased. It would mean that the variable is taken for exogenous, while in fact it is endogenous. Instead of a one-way traffic between the explanatory and the dependent variable, changes in the latter would also affect the former. In the case under consideration this could arise, for example, if changes in current sales were reflected in current advertising expenditure. Even if this were true to some extent, the single equation least squares approach might still yield satisfactory results. The degree of the specification error (the error of assuming that there is no correlation between the disturbance term and the independent variable—as opposed to the ever present sampling error) will be relatively small when the degree of correlation between the "exogenous" variable and the disturbance is small. It will also be small when the regression analysis accounts for a substantial part of the variation in the endogenous variable.[1]

The condition of linear independence among the disturbance terms will be fulfilled when these follow an autoregressive relationship of the form

$$(2.10) \qquad\qquad u_t = u_{t-1} + \epsilon_t$$

where ϵ is a serially independent random variable with a finite, constant variance. If the error term in Koyck's model is defined as

$$u_t - \kappa u_{t-1} = v_t \quad \text{and} \quad \kappa = \lambda$$

then

$$(2.11) \qquad\qquad v_t = \epsilon_t$$

If $\kappa = \lambda$, it also follows that S_{t-1} and v_t are uncorrelated. The assumption that random disturbances are generated by a simple Markov process is frequently encountered in econometric work.[2] It reflects the widely held opinion that positive serial correlation is to be found very often in economic time series. Thus, what at first seems a handicap may

---

[1] H. Wold and P. Faxer, "On the Specification Error in Regression Analysis," *Annals of Mathematical Statistics*, **XXVIII**, No. 1 (1957), 265–67.

[2] Klein, *op. cit.*, p. 85.

actually turn out to be an advantage of the Koyck model, depending upon how close κ is to λ.[1]

It is worth mentioning the Bayesian position on this point. The Bayesian approach implies that the inferential import of the data is contained in the likelihood function. If we assume that the dependent variable is normally distributed and generated by an autoregressive scheme, the likelihood function is the same as it is for ordinary regressions.[2] In particular, the usual least-squares analyses will then yield the needed parameters of the posterior distribution, given a jointly diffuse prior distribution. In the case under investigation, however, the normality assumption was not made, so there was no commitment to a particular likelihood function.

Certain other potential advantages of the distributed lag model will presently be mentioned. However, first it should be emphasized that beyond and above all the statistical and managerial considerations— yet incorporating them all—there loom these fundamental questions: does Koyck's model of distributed lags *express* better than any heretofore employed implicit models the mechanism by which advertising influences sales over long stretches of time? Perhaps even more importantly, can it *forecast* sales from current and past advertising expenditures well enough to be useful to advertisers? It is the task of this dissertation to try and provide the answers to these questions. This it will do by examining the statistical *fit* of the model to a set of actual data and by looking at its *predictive* ability.

The "traditional" models that embody the concept of distributed lags typically use a considerable number of (lagged) independent variables while the simple Koyck model uses only one lagged and one non-lagged exogenous variable. If this substantially simpler model were to give nearly as good a picture of reality as the more complicated ones, it would be advantageous to employ it. For instance, the fact that Koyck's model does not use a variable in several lagged versions (e.g., A_t, A_{t-1}, A_{t-2}, etc.) means that it is less exposed to the dangers of multicol-

---

[1] Marc Nerlove, "Estimates of Elasticities of Supply of Selected Agricultural Commodities," *Journal of Farm Economics*, **XXXVIII** (May, 1956), 496–509.

[2] "Thus in constructing the likelihood function, i.e., in making inferences from a particular series, there is no difference at all between the autoregressive case and the ordinary regression case . . . . We may contrast this approach with that of current theory, which treats the autoregressive case as being distinct from the ordinary case." G. A. Barnard, G. M. Jenkins, C. B. Winsten, "Likelihood Inference and Time Series (With Discussion)," *Journal of the Royal Statistical Society, Series A (General)* (Part 3, 1962), pp. 336–37.

linearity than the other models. Errors of measurement in data can become greatly magnified and distort seriously parameter estimates if extreme collinearity is present. Also, high levels of intercorrelation are reflected in high standard errors of the net regression coefficients and this tends to mean lowered reliability for the individual parameter estimates.

The final remark of predominantly statistical nature concerns Koyck's geometric distribution of lags, insofar as it is one of the many possible distributions with discrete lags. Mundlak suggests that there may be an aggregation problem when the length of the period chosen for observation (such as a quarter) differs from the "true" length of the adjustment period (such as a month).[1]

From the economic and managerial points of view models incorporating distributed lags give an investment perspective to advertising outlays. Koyck's model presents, however, aspects of a short-term nature as well. Some of its short- and long-run facets will now be explored. The discussion is based, without loss of generality, on (2.9) where the "geometric" reaction gets underway in the very first period.

For ease of reference write again (2.9), omitting the random disturbance:

$$S_t = a + \alpha A_t + \lambda S_{t-1}$$

The marginal effect of advertising on sales in the short run is obtained by differentiating S_t with respect to A_t. Thus $\hat{\alpha}$ is its estimate. The equilibrium concept is resorted to in order to bring out the long-run effect. As the firm approaches its optimal activity level there is no tendency for sales to move away from an equilibrium level S_e. In such circumstances S_e tends to equate S_t and S_{t-1}:

(2.12) $$S_e = a + \alpha A_t + \lambda S_e$$

(2.13) $$\frac{dS_e}{dA_t} = \frac{\alpha}{1 - \lambda}$$

Estimates of the expression $\alpha/1 - \lambda$ thus represent the long-term marginal sales effect of advertising. It will be noted that this expression also stands for the sum to infinity of the convergent geometric series formed by the coefficients of A_t.

Short- and long-run advertising elasticities of sales, or of sales revenue, are obtained when the corresponding marginal sales effects are multi-

---

[1] Yair Mundlak, "Aggregation Over Time in Distributed Lag Models," *International Economic Review*, **II** (May, 1961), 154–63.

plied by the ratio av A_t/av S_t, where av stands for the average sample period amount.[1] The marginal rate of return on the invested advertising dollar can be discovered by a simple discounting procedure. Recall the series

$$\alpha A_t + \alpha\lambda A_{t-1} + \alpha\lambda^2 A_{t-2} + \cdots$$

and put A_i ($i = t, t - 1, \ldots$) equal to \$1. Which rate of discounting will bring the series of *net* future receipts to equality with the increase in current outlay, the present value of which is \$1? (2.15) provides an answer.

(2.14)
$$\$1 = c\alpha + \frac{c\alpha\lambda}{1 + r} + \frac{c\alpha\lambda^2}{(1 + r)^2} + \cdots$$

$$= c\alpha \left(1 + \frac{\lambda}{1 + r} + \frac{\lambda^2}{(1 + r)^2} + \cdots \right)$$

$$= c\alpha \left(\frac{1}{1 - \dfrac{\lambda}{1 + r}} \right); \quad 0 < c < 1$$

(2.15)
$$r = \frac{c\alpha - \lambda - 1}{1 - c}$$

where c is 1 *minus* all costs, except advertising, as per cent of sales.

By way of a "lemma," another insight into the investment aspects of the model can be gained.[2] Assume that this period's sales, S_t, are a linear function of an advertising capital, a_t^*, accumulated over the past. In turn, this capital can be viewed as capital accumulated up to the beginning of the current period, suitably depreciated over this current period and comprising this period's advertising expenditure as well. Thus:

(2.16)
$$S_t = k + \alpha a_t^*$$

where

$$a_t^* = (1 - r)a_{t-1}^* + A_t$$

---

[1] Since double-logarithmic scales are not employed here, the advertising elasticity of sales changes with every change in A_t and S_t. It is a convention in econometrics to use the sample means of the variables to compute "average" elasticity. The alternative, which is av $(dS/dA \times A/S)$, is not a point on the demand schedule.

[2] I am indebted to Professor L. Telser for this suggestion. A similar perspective is thoroughly explored in Arrow and Nerlove, *op. cit.*

Now multiply (2.16) by $(1 - r)$, lag it one period and subtract the result from the original equation to get

(2.17) $\qquad S_t = kr + (1 - r) S_{t-1} + \alpha[a_t^* - (1 - r)a_{t-1}^*]$

As the expression in the square brackets represents A_t, here is Koyck's model written in a slightly different way. This seems a good way to bring out, among other things, the fact that the rate of depreciation r, is $1 - \lambda$.[1]

A remark on the meaning of the independent variable S_{t-1} may be in order. It can be viewed as representing a weighted moving average of all past advertising outlays. It can also be interpreted more simply as a measure of past sales which encompasses a host of variables that molded consumer's habits. If its inclusion in the regression equation is chiefly responsible for a high coefficient of multiple regression, this can be interpreted to mean that the cumulative action of past advertising outlays and other influences is more important in shaping current sales than is current advertising.

---

[1] Beyond a certain point of time the addition of earlier A_is has but a slight effect on S_t. To find the length of time required for, say, 95 per cent of the total effect to occur, the following procedure is helpful. Remembering that convergent geometric series are dealt with here, write $S_n/S_\infty \geqslant .95$, or $1 - \lambda^n \geqslant .95$, where S is the sum of n (or of an infinite) number of terms of the geometric progression. Solving for n,

$$n \leqslant \log (.05)/\log (\lambda).$$

The result indicates the number of periods that will elapse, on the average, before the invested advertising dollar loses 95 per cent of its (gross) revenue—generating power.

CHAPTER 3

The Case of Lydia Pinkham

While only lagged sales revenue and advertising expenditures were used as exogenous variables in the exposition of the model, the multiple regression analysis can be expanded by taking into account additional factors, such as trend or price. Some of these variables could even be lagged in Koyck's fashion. Yet keeping the analysis as simple as possible has much merit. Fortunately, there exists a case in the annals of advertising (and of American folklore) which invites a fairly straightforward test of Koyck's model.

In the years 1935–37 a bitter court litigation between two factions of the family-owned Lydia E. Pinkham Medicine Company in Lynn, Massachusetts produced a complete record of the firm's annual advertising expenditures and sales over the period 1908 to 1935. Thanks to the attendant publicity, a *Printer's Ink* reporter was present in court and recorded the data, which were published in the December 10, 1936 issue of that periodical. Subsequently they were reprinted in a Harvard case book.[1]

Data relating the sales and advertising of a product over many years are very rarely available to students. For this reason the availability of the Pinkham data moved the Committee on Price Determination of the National Bureau of Economic Research to recommend in 1943 that they be subjected to intensive analysis.[2] Nobody took up the suggestion,

---

[1] Neil H. Borden, *Problems in Advertising* (New York: McGraw-Hill, Inc., 1937).

[2] Committee on Price Determination for the Conference on Price Research, *Cost Behavior and Price Policy* (New York: National Bureau of Economic Research, 1943), p. 212.

although Lydia Pinkham became the subject of several Harvard advertising cases that were published later on and contained much that was interesting.[1] The writer was fortunate in being able to secure the full cooperation of the company's management and, as a consequence, obtained a generous amount of data and information covering the period 1907–1960.

Lydia Pinkham's Vegetable Compound, the chief product of the Pinkham Company to this day, is one of the legendary proprietary medicines that attained fame before the turn of this century. A pioneering user of intensive advertising, it was attacked by muckrakers, mockingly serenaded by college students, and pursued by the Federal Trade Commission. The company and the product have been the subject of many articles in various periodicals, including the *Journal of the American Medical Association* and *Life*. The latest of them, appearing in 1957 in a specialized medical periodical, carries a fairly comprehensive bibliography.[2] An informal history of the company was written by Jean Burton and published in 1949.[3] However, by far the richest source of information is a privately printed and circulated work by a grandson of the founder, Charles H. Pinkham.[4] According to the company's present management, it is also the most reliable written record of the firm's activities up to 1953.

Since there are relatively many descriptions of the company and the product available—of which perhaps the published Harvard cases are those most easily accessible to students of business—the history of Lydia Pinkham will be only briefly recounted here. Certain important episodes or aspects of the company's operations will be treated more fully in subsequent chapters to provide a background for the statistical and economic analysis. In Chap. 4 special attention will be given to changes in such important variables as price and copy policy. These changes will be specifically related to the behavior of the company's sales.

Lydia Pinkham's Vegetable Compound was first brewed and prepared by the lady in question as a home remedy for her friends. The compound, a herbal extract in alcoholic solution, was considered to be

---

[1] Neil H. Borden, *Advertising*: *Text and Cases* (Homewood, Ill.: Richard D. Irwin, Inc., 1949 and 1959).

[2] Lee Strohl, "Ladies of Lynn—Emphasis on One," *Surgery, Gynecology and Obstetrics*, December, 1957, pp. 755–69.

[3] *Lydia Pinkham Is Her Name* (New York: Farrar, Straus & Co., 1949).

[4] *Advertising, Volume I* (Lynn, Mass.: Lydia E. Pinkham Medicine Company, 1953).

effective against "women's weakness." This condition is more precisely described as either menopausal malaise or menstrual pain. The first commercial sale of the medicine was made in 1873. Twelve years later, with production removed from the kitchen stove, annual sales of the Compound reached $500,000. The profits were being reinvested immediately into advertising campaigns of unprecedented intensity, making the kindly face of Lydia Pinkham (reproduced to this day on the package carton) known across the land. With commercial success came the expansion of copy claims. The medicine was now a sure cure for "the falling and displacement of the womb, ovarian troubles, tumors and cancerous humours; also for faintness, headache, general debility and for kidney complaints of either sex."

Having reached a peak of almost $1.5 million annually at the turn of the century, sales started to fall despite an advertising expenditure occasionally exceeding 60 per cent of sales. By 1908 they declined to $920,000.[1] At that time the company sold the liquid to the trade for $87.32 per gross of bottles. While drug wholesalers accounted for the bulk of sales, retail druggists could also order directly provided they exceeded a certain modest minimum amount. Resale prices were not maintained and Pinkham's management successfully opposed pressure for price maintenance from wholesale and retail associations. Indeed, the popularity of the Vegetable Compound made it at the time a widely used loss leader.

During the entire period under consideration, that is from 1907 to 1960, the company employed no salesmen. The last vestiges of quantity and cash discounts disappeared in 1917, and advertising to consumers has to all intents and purposes carried the entire burden of the marketing effort. Since advertising was practically the only selling expense, it is not surprising that its ratio to current sales was very high, dipping only exceptionally below 40 per cent. Until the 1930's almost 85 per cent of the advertising appropriation went to newspapers, the rest being spent mostly on pamphlets and correspondence with consumers. Direct product substitutes were giving little competition and the company's advertising reflects this quite clearly: the copy was not preoccupied with competitors, but aimed at the stimulation of "primary" demand. Some sales were being made abroad, chiefly in Canada, reaching as much as 15 per cent of the company's total.

---

[1] The published court records of sales and advertising expenditures start with the year 1908. Detailed data were made available by management from 1907 on. Yearly figures for most of the pre-1907 period appear in *ibid.*

The shares of the company are held in equal part by the descendants of Lydia Pinkham's two surviving children, Arthur Pinkham and Aroline Gove. This equal division of ownership led to some mistrust between the two families and consequently to the adoption of rather unusual company by-laws. They specify in minute detail the powers and responsibilities of executive officers representing the Pinkham and Gove stocks and, in essence, require a unanimity of opinion on important decisions.[1] Only one particular feature of the by-laws needs to be noted: Section 3 of Article VIII forbids the accumulation of net surplus to an amount exceeding $1 million. This provision clearly limits long-term capital expenditure planning.

After years of decline, sales turned up again in 1909 and continued to grow, as is delineated in Table 1 and Figure 2. In 1914 two changes occurred. The solid content of the liquid compound was increased sevenfold under prodding from the Internal Revenue Department which threatened to tax the medicine as an alcoholic beverage. Also statements on labels, wrappers and inserts had to be modified as they were found

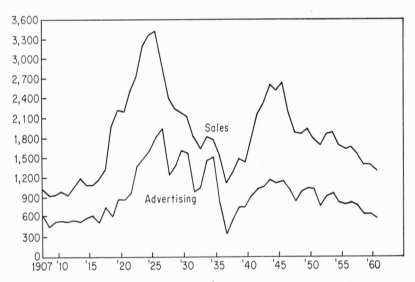

Fig. 2. Sales and advertising of Lydia E. Pinkham Medicine Company, 1907–1960

---

[1] It is said that the Harvard Law School uses the Lydia Pinkham case (recorded during the 1935–37 litigation) as the perfect example of legally devised corporate deadlock. Real difficulties did not arise, however, until the mid-twenties.

TABLE 1. DOMESTIC SALES AND ADVERTISING OF LYDIA E. PINKHAM MEDICINE COMPANY
1907–1960

(in $000)

Year	Sales	Advertising
1907	1016	608
1908	921	451
1909	934	529
1910	976	543
1911	930	525
1912	1052	549
1913	1184	525
1914	1089	578
1915	1087	609
1916	1154	504
1917	1330	752
1918	1980	613
1919	2223	862
1920	2203	866
1921	2514	1016
1922	2726	1360
1923	3185	1482
1924	3351	1608
1925	3438	1800
1926	2917	1941
1927	2359	1229
1928	2240	1373
1929	2196	1611
1930	2111	1568
1931	1806	983
1932	1644	1046
1933	1814	1453
1934	1770	1504
1935	1518	807
1936	1103	339
1937	1266	562
1938	1473	745
1939	1423	749
1940	1767	862
1941	2161	1034
1942	2336	1054
1943	2602	1164
1944	2518	1102
1945	2637	1145
1946	2177	1012
1947	1920	836
1948	1910	941
1949	1984	981
1950	1787	974
1951	1689	766
1952	1866	920
1953	1896	964
1954	1684	811
1955	1633	789
1956	1657	802
1957	1569	770
1958	1390	639
1959	1387	644
1960	1289	564

Source: Company records.

false and misleading by the Food and Drug Administration. Claims of vast curative powers were therefore sharply reduced and even advertising copy had to be toned down. From the beginning of 1916 the liquid tonic's alcoholic content stood at about 15 per cent, a reduction of about 3 per cent from the previous level. In November 1917, the price of the Compound was increased by almost 25 per cent to $108 a gross, or 75 cents a bottle, including freight charges as before. At the same time all discounts were eliminated. The next price change was announced on November 25, 1929. From December 15 on, a gross of bottles was to be sold for $120, an increase of 11 per cent. Buyers could stock up at the old price.[1]

Until 1925 sales continued to grow. In that year they reached the highest level in the history of the company—almost $3.5 million. Two events occurred then which influenced the subsequent fortunes of the company.

In November of 1925 the Food and Drug Administration ordered the company to cease and desist from continuing to use its then current label claims. From the beginning of 1926, labels and other printed material distributed with the Compound recommended it only as a vegetable tonic. Advertising copy had to follow suit, and advertising claims that the product acted directly upon the female organs were abandoned. Sales immediatedly declined.

Miss Lydia Gove, a granddaughter of the founder, became a director of the company in 1925. Although she was assistant treasurer of the company, Lydia Gove was primarily interested in advertising. Her impetuous and headstrong nature asserted itself successfully against opposition and from 1926 on she dominated the advertising department. When James T. Wetherald, the agent who handled Pinkham's advertising for four decades, died in 1927, Miss Gove took upon herself even the preparation of copy. The growing difficulties of the company, stemming from the continued decline of sales, did nothing to alleviate the Pinkham–Gove controversy, further inflamed by Lydia Gove's determination not to cut the advertising budget. When in 1934 the advertising-sales ratio reached 85 per cent, the president of the company, Arthur Pinkham, decided to put a stop to such extravagant expenditure. He also determined to engage the services of an outside advertising agency, instead of relying on the house agency that the company set up after Wetherald's death.

---

[1] The 1930 sales figure was adjusted upward by management in order to take into account the rush of orders following the announcement of the price increase. These orders were mostly at the expense of the 1930 sales.

When Lydia Gove and her mother declined to acquiesce in the choice of a New York agency by withholding, in their respective capacities of assistant treasurer and treasurer, authorization to pay the agency's bills, the Pinkhams sued. In July, 1937 the Supreme Court of Massachusetts upheld the right of the president to run the company.[1] From that time on a truce prevailed between the two families.

After the start of litigation, advertising expenditures were drastically reduced. While in the first seven months of 1935 advertising outlays amounted to $714,000, they ran to only $127,000 during the twelve months starting with August, 1935. In 1936 sales had reached their lowest point in twenty years. At the end of that year advertising expenditures were again being restored to their customary level and sales began to climb. Massive use of radio was experimented with for the first time in 1936. In 1937 Vitamin B1 was added to the tonic and iron to the Vegetable Compound in tablet form to bring them "up to date."

In 1938 the Federal Trade Commission raised new objections to the company's advertising copy. The company had to restrict its copy claims, while it argued about them with the FTC for two years. Finally, with the help of medical consultants, it was able to demonstrate the possibility that the active herbal ingredients contained estrogenic substances, as well as uterine stimulants and sedatives.[2] From 1941 on, the Commission permitted the company to advertise its products for the "relief of symptoms associated with and caused by menstrual aberrations and by menopause." After that copy stronger than anything since 1925 could be written again.

Sales expanded from $1.1 million in 1936 to $2.6 million in 1945. Although the liquid tonic remained the most popular item, sales of tablets containing the Compound grew in importance. In 1943 they accounted for about $500,000, or a quarter of total sales revenue. In 1956 almost half of total dollar sales was accounted for by the tablets. Other company products, such as liver pills, laxatives and aspirin rarely exceeded 1 per cent of total sales.

The postwar increases in raw material and other costs brought about two changes in the price of the liquid tonic in 1947. On May 1 it went up to $11 a dozen and on December 27 it further increased to $12 a dozen, after prior notification to the trade. The $14\frac{1}{2}$ ounce bottle of tonic now

---

[1] *Massachusetts Reports*, **CCXCVIII** (Boston: Wright and Potter Printing Co., 1940).

[2] Laboratory biochemical and clinical research did not substantiate these claims until several years later.

sold 20 per cent higher than in 1930. Tablets continued to sell at $10 a dozen bottles, each containing 72 tablets, until 1950, when the price was lowered by 33 cents. Price increases in 1956 brought the tablets up to $11.[1]

Under pressure from the trade, the company adopted the policy of recommending minimum fair trade prices at the beginning of 1948. By March, 1949 fair trade contracts were signed in all the 45 states having fair trade laws. The liquid (or the bottle containing 72 tablets) was to be sold at retail for no less than $1.39. This was increased to $1.49 in August 1954. A subsequent survey did not find any marked differences in retail prices paid by women in fair trade and non-fair trade states. The company made no attempt to enforce the minimum price.

A minor change was made in the formula of the Vegetable Compound in 1951. In 1952 the alcohol content of the liquid tonic was decreased from 15 to 13.5 per cent. Its bitter and rather unpleasant taste was left unchanged. Also in that year labels and cartons were "cleaned up" and given a more modern look, but retaining the founder's face as the dominant feature. By 1953 the liquid compound was being offered in its traditional $14\frac{1}{2}$ ounce bottle as well as in a 7 ounce bottle, while tablets sold in bottles containing quantities of 24, 72, or 250.

By 1943, the company was back to an almost exclusive use of news-papers as its advertising medium. The postwar period saw considerable switching from newspapers to radio to magazines and even to television. In the last three or four years of the period under consideration the pattern reminds one of the early 'forties—about two-thirds of money spent on newspapers and one-third on spot radio.

This brief chronological narrative provides a general context for those aspects of the case which must be studied separately and in greater detail in the next chapter. Before turning to it, a survey is in order of the advantages that the Pinkham case offers for a quantitative study of advertising effectiveness by means of time series analysis.

As was already stressed, it is quite unusual for a long time series of a firm's advertising and sales data to be available. Yet despite the many years which the Pinkham data covers, the universe, of which the observa-tions can be considered to be a sample, remained relatively stable. The product, in taste, form and action, is essentially the same as it was fifty years ago. The exclusive reliance on advertising remains unchanged. No close competitor appeared on the scene. Even the heavy use of news-papers as an advertising medium still prevails. To be sure, there have

---

[1] Price changes are summarized in tabular form in Chap. 4.

been some changes in price, character of copy, and in that catch-all, tastes. But these changes are not unduly numerous and can be coped with statistically.

By the beginning of this century the Vegetable Compound was already a mature product, not subject to the vagaries a newly launched product usually undergoes. The company, throughout the whole period, spent a very high proportion of its sales (40–60 per cent) on advertising. Furthermore, it did not employ many of the customary tools of marketing action: a sales force, credit, discounts, frequent changes in package, point of purchase efforts, special offerings, etc. There is thus no reason to doubt, as there is in so many demand studies, that advertising had indeed influenced the company's sales.

The product itself had no close substitutes. Competitors' marketing action is therefore not a complicating factor to be coped with—especially as regards rival advertising and pricing policies. Other factors that add to the simplicity of the ultimate quantitative analysis will be discussed in the next chapter.

Finally, consumer surveys carried out by the company (see Chap. 5) indicated that the Vegetable Compound commands a lasting allegiance on the part of many of its users. This is one of the circumstances from which a lagged advertising effect may be inferred.

CHAPTER 4

Preliminaries to
Regression Analysis

The next step is to prepare, in this chapter, the way for the multiple regression analysis required to explore the model of cumulative effects. Variables, believed to have a systematic effect on the sales of the company, must be settled upon. A suitable length of the unit time period to be used must also be selected.

However, at the very start consideration must be given to the units in which the two most important variables, sales and advertising, are to be measured. It is proposed to measure both sales and advertising in (thousands of) current dollars.

The character of the Pinkham data makes it inconvenient to measure sales in physical units. There is no continuous record over the entire period of the number of units sold. Furthermore, from the 'forties on, tablets take a growing share of total sales. However, the liquid tonic and tablets are advertised either jointly or separately with no visible and consistent pattern of distinctive appeals or intensity. It thus seems reasonable to adopt sales revenue as the dependent variable.[1]

---

[1] It can be shown that the elasticity of sales revenue with respect to advertising expenditure is the same as that of physical unit sales with respect to advertising expenditure if no change occurred in price. Let the advertising elasticity of sales revenue be expressed as

$$E = \frac{d(pq)}{da} \frac{a}{pq}$$

where p is price, q is quantity sold, their product is sales revenue and a is advertising expenditure. Then, if the differentiation is carried out and no change in price is postulated

$$E = \left(\frac{dp}{p} + \frac{dq}{q} \right) \frac{a}{da} = \frac{dq}{da} \frac{a}{q} \quad \text{if} \quad dp = 0$$

It is more convenient to express the advertising variable in monetary units than in physical units. The records of the company do not show, over the entire period of 53 years, details of space or time purchased in the two most important advertising media employed: newspapers and radio (spot). Even if they did, however, it would still be very difficult to select a satisfactory physical unit of advertising and to measure its volume.

Consider newspapers first. A plausible, if crude, unit in which to measure advertising volume in this medium is one agate line of advertisement sent to one million circulation. However, in order to determine how many millines of advertising were carried by a newspaper, its circulation must be known. Unfortunately, the Audit Bureau of Circulations, which reports on newspapers, has been in existence only since the mid-twenties. Many of the small-town newspapers which carried the bulk of Pinkham's advertising were not audited until much later.

"Gross potential audience reached" is often employed as a physical index of radio advertising.[1] Nevertheless, the count of the average number of families who listen to a station during a given time of the day was not undertaken until 1946, when it was pioneered by the Bureau of Broadcast Measurement. Even if it were possible to measure Pinkham's advertising volume in newspapers and radio in such units, there would arise the rather difficult problem of making them comparable to each other.

Further, top management is not primarily interested in knowing the marginal *physical* product of the firm's advertising dollar, provided it can discover the value of its marginal revenue product. For present purposes, monetary units are a satisfactory means of measurement.

The employment of a physical index of advertising volume would, however, avoid the potential problem of the changing purchasing power of the advertising dollar. Not much is known about that problem. What evidence there is indicates, that with rising costs for space and time, media productivity increased as well. There is thus no indication of a

---

[1] The Audience Concept Committee of the Advertising Research Foundation set up six levels of media and vehicle evaluation. Physical distribution—a physical count of the publications, devices or sets that can carry advertising messages—is the first and least satisfactory level. The milline corresponds to this level. Gross potential audience corresponds to the next level, designated as total audience and defined as the number of people exposed to a medium's editorial, entertainment or advertising material. For the other four levels see Albert W. Frey, *Advertising* (New York: The Ronald Press Company, 1961), p. 265.

clear trend in the purchasing power of Pinkham's advertising expenditures over most of the relevant period.[1]

As with advertising outlays, so with sales revenue: there is no satisfactory deflator available (there was not even a wholesale price index in existence in 1910, not to speak of an index of drug product prices). It thus seemed best to relate sales revenue in current dollars to advertising revenue in current dollars in the regression analysis that was undertaken.

The management of Lydia Pinkham made available monthly advertising expenditure and sales figures which, in principle, offered a choice of the period to be employed in the time series analysis. Periods of a month, a quarter and a year were all considered and the year was chosen as the most suitable unit. The reasoning leading to the choice had to take account of the aggregation problem which can arise when the postulated adjustment period is not the same as the true one; of the seasonal fluctuations of the series, and of certain other practical problems.

Consider the miscellaneous problems first. Many variables that can plausibly be thought of as influencing sales of the proprietary medicine are available only in a yearly form. A good example is consumer disposable income where estimates are available only on a yearly basis in the early years of the period under consideration here.

Monthly or quarterly data are also likely to be more prone to errors of observation. While no precise example can be adduced as far as the secondary data are concerned, there is a straightforward one in the Pinkham observations. The advertising expenditures are posted to the months during which the advertisements are supposed to appear, rather than to the months during which they are billed for. This procedure is subject to a margin of error, but it is an improvement on the method used in the earlier part of the period, when advertising expenses were recorded at the time when they were billed or credited. One of the curious results of this method showed advertising outlays incurred in December, 1916 as minus $2,993.

----

[1] "In the three major kinds of printed mass media—metropolitan newspapers, consumer magazines and business papers—the cost of buying equivalent space-circulation units, expressed in constant dollars is only two-thirds to one-half of the 1929 cost, and is on par with the costs of the early 1920's. These conclusions are based upon an analysis of twelve major metropolitian newspapers, fourteen consumer magazines and ten business papers over a thirty-eight year period." Kenneth H. Myers, "Have We a Decline in Advertising Appropriations?" *Journal of Marketing*, **XXIII** (April, 1959), 372.

Monthly and quarterly sales and advertising outlays exhibit very strong seasonal swings. So marked are the seasonal fluctuations that it was considered advisable to remove them before subjecting the series to regression analysis. A typical extract from the full series is graphically represented in Fig. 3. Monthly sales and advertising data from January 1954 to July 1960 are shown. August sales observations are heavily marked to draw attention to the fact that there is no stable pattern in the seasonal fluctuations.

The need for de-seasonalization may be clear, but the means to satisfy it are less than adequate. Also, de-seasonalization may bring in its wake some unwanted consequences.

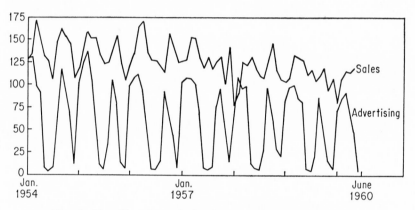

Fig. 3. Monthly sales and advertising expenditures of Lydia E. Pinkham Company, January 1954–July 1960 (in $000)

Removing seasonal influences from the data may introduce serial correlation into the series or shift the timing of their rises and falls and so disguise a relationship between two time series.[1] Thus if, for instance, sales are subjected to a sharp one-period disturbance, the moving average process of seasonal adjustment will spread the disturbance over several subsequent periods and introduce correlation between the successive observations. When, as another example, the dependent variable follows closely the explanatory variable whose intensity is deliberately manipulated to exploit some underlying seasonal pattern, seasonal adjustment will tend to mask the causal relationship between the two.

---

[1] W. Allen Wallis and Harry V. Roberts, *Statistics—A New Approach* (New York: The Free Press of Glencoe, Inc., 1956), pp. 578–79.

TABLE 2. ORIGINAL AND SEASONALLY ADJUSTED U.S. MONTHLY SALES AND ADVERTISING
EXPENDITURES OF LYDIA PINKHAM MEDICINE COMPANY JANUARY 1954 TO JULY 1960

	Original Figures (in $00)		Seasonally Adjusted Figures (in $00)	
	Advertising	Sales	Advertising	Sales
Jan. 1954	1280	1295	828	1451
	1350	1318	718	1387
	982	1728	468	1426
	919	1539	556	1390
	87	1324	351	1311
	39	1264	680	1362
	72	1169	570	1337
Aug.	467	1479	582	1462
	1170	1631	775	1517
	917	1546	600	1348
	701	1459	1019	1476
	128	1087	755	1366
Jan. 1955	1014	1171	607	1343
	1274	1406	682	1478
	1388	1619	886	1341
	1071	1508	716	1360
	537	1521	741	1487
	123	1341	726	1422
	60	1247	567	1376
Aug.	351	1262	539	1277
	1061	1419	680	1336
	791	1558	433	1259
	138	1222	433	1259
	77	1053	650	1261
Jan. 1956	1000	1242	638	1431
	1182	1361	630	1437
	1225	1660	735	1426
	936	1717	590	1570
	625	1371	769	1316
	60	1293	624	1357
	61	1285	578	1376
Aug.	169	1210	430	1256
	946	1142	579	1090
	1306	1586	1057	1402
	426	1441	698	1497
	88	1262	606	1400
Jan. 1957	1104	1267	787	1472
	1093	1278	581	1357
	1080	1544	602	1344
	1012	1534	674	1388

TABLE 2. ORIGINAL AND SEASONALLY ADJUSTED U.S. MONTHLY SALES AND ADVERTISING
EXPENDITURES OF LYDIA PINKHAM MEDICINE COMPANY JANUARY 1954 TO JULY 1960
(*Cont.*)

	Original Figures (in $00)		Seasonally Adjusted Figures (in $00)	
	Advertising	Sales	Advertising	Sales
	745	1332	829	1257
	78	1200	604	1246
	66	1314	593	1367
Aug.	94	1180	428	1257
	774	1264	421	1243
	971	1318	756	1142
	536	1018	785	1093
	150	1438	613	1506
Jan. 1958	580	772	308	993
	1121	902	649	984
	974	1265	508	1099
	1002	1229	673	1085
	138	1318	162	1222
	72	1195	559	1224
	59	1105	595	1119
Aug.	270	1095	667	1204
	986	1298	647	1308
	673	1482	492	1312
	304	1163	530	1258
	209	1072	618	1069
Jan. 1959	838	1052	611	1290
	994	1102	562	1188
	1020	1355	566	1223
	865	1323	544	1180
	819	1296	783	1179
	83	1127	532	1139
	56	1170	602	1145
Aug.	224	1059	703	1199
	881	1116	557	1156
	436	1214	289	1053
	160	966	364	1080
	68	1089	422	1016
Jan. 1960	749	814	567	1068
	857	1087	465	1182
	898	1180	456	1082
	705	1167	392	1025
	489	1210	392	1073
June	59	1092	469	1087

Source: Company records.

A quick check of the Pinkham monthly figures is not particularly revealing. Table 2 shows a series of 78 monthly sales and advertising figures before de-seasonalization (Fig. 3 is based on these) and after it.[1] There are 40 runs up and down in the original sales series and 48 runs in the de-seasonalized sales series. Approximate corresponding standard normal variables are −3.0 and −.9. The sales and advertising series show 34 runs up or down in the same direction before seasonal adjustment. After adjustment there are 32 runs in the same direction and thus no apparent effect from de-seasonalization.

While the method of seasonal adjustment employed for the period 1954–1960 is quite elaborate, it does not come close to the sophistication of the electronic computer program for the seasonal adjustment of economic time series prepared by the National Bureau of Economic Research.[2] This program was used to adjust the Pinkham data covering the years 1908 to 1935, but it was then decided not to use its results for the reasons outlined above and, also, because no matter how elaborate and "objective" the smoothing methods may be, they still contain a large arbitrary element. The growing dissatisfaction with the existing methods of de-composition of time-series has led recently to applications of spectral analysis to business-cycle and other economic studies. (Spectral analysis being, however, still in the pioneering stage in economics, it was not deemed advisable to apply it to the Pinkham data.)

------

[1] The smoothing of the series was accomplished in two steps. First, the series was de-seasonalized by the "difference from moving average method." After plotting each month's adjusted observations (all Januaries, e.g.), it was noticed that the data exhibited trends. Therefore a more complicated procedure was adopted. It is probably better to describe every single step of the final method used, including even the "difference from moving average" phase:

Step 1—original observation
Step 2—12 months' moving total
Step 3—2 months' moving total of (2)
Step 4—centered 12 months' moving average (3) ÷ 24
Step 5—original observations minus (4) equal to "preliminary" months
Step 6—a least squares regression of "preliminary" months (e.g., all Januaries) on time. Time is expressed as −3 in 1954, as 0 in 1957, as 3 in 1960 etc.
Step 7—the regression equations yield least squares estimates for each desired period.
Step 8—the least squares estimates (7) are subtracted from the original observations to give the final, deseasonalized figures.

[2] This program is described in Julius Shiskin, "Electronic Computers and Business Indicators," *Journal of Business*, **XXX** (October, 1957), 219–67.

The following quotation from an article by Oskar Morgenstern, in which he expresses his uneasiness about the prevalent methods of time-series de-composition, leads from the problems of de-seasonalization to the consideration of lags:

> For the same set of series there may prevail another lead-lag relation when seasonal fluctuations are considered than when their trends are investigated. Trends are more closely related to trends than trends to seasonals, each set of variations having a structure of its own, which needs to be explored, but for which purpose the usual techniques appear to be inadequate. In other words, the lag may or may not depend on the particular frequency observed.[1]

It follows that an inquiry into the "true" length of the unit adjustment period (unit lag) is affected by a prior smoothing of the time-series. If, in the search for the correct lag, time periods shorter than a year are considered, the violence of their seasonal fluctuations requires that they be adjusted first. But this adjustment, because of the imperfect way in which it was brought about, is likely to distort the "true" length of the lag.[2]

There are no a priori grounds which would lead to a preference for a particular unit adjustment period, such as a month, a quarter or a year. For instance, it may be suspected that there is an institutional lag due to the way the measurements are taken. Monthly sales figures are recorded as orders leave the factory, while monthly advertising figures are posted when the actual advertisements appear. It could thus be reasonably expected that if advertising is increased and sales respond immediately, the cushioning action of retail and wholesale stocks will delay the appearance of orders at factory level. Thus a certain lag, say of two months, due entirely to the institutional set-up of the trade, would appear between advertising and sales and contribute to the establishment of a unit reaction period. But for years the company has almost stopped advertising in late spring and early summer and during two or three months around Christmas. It is difficult to believe that distributors have not learned to anticipate such seasonal swings.

---

[1] Oskar Morgenstern, "A New Look at Economic Time Series," *L'industria* (Milano, Italy: 1961), No. 3, pp. 333–34.

[2] Reference is made again to the article by Mundlak which shows the unpleasant possibilities inherent in the wrong choice of a unit time period for the analysis of distributed lags, *loc. cit.*

The fact that the individual consumer up to a certain age is typically subject to a monthly menstrual cycle loses its significance when large numbers are considered and when it is realized that the compound is also taken for other, non-menstrual, ills such as change of life.

It was therefore necessary to fall back on such statistical evidence as was available. The seasonally adjusted monthly data for 1954 to 1960 which appear in Table 2 were subjected to several regression analyses.

If a month were a proper period for analysis, it would be expected that some kind of consistent pattern between monthly advertising and monthly sales would emerge. It could be, for instance, that advertising and sales during the same month are most highly correlated and that this relationship weakens thereafter. Or that the concurrent relation is very weak, but is more clearly visible as the lag between past advertising and current sales grows. Monthly sales were therefore correlated with monthly advertising expenditures incurred during the same month and during each of the preceding twelve months. The resulting simple correlation coefficients, shown in Fig. 4, do not exhibit any discernible regularities.

Restricted access to computer facilities prevented, unfortunately, the calculation of *multiple* regression estimates with the thirteen months as independent variables. Thus the *net* relation (assuming that no other but advertising forces were present) between monthly sales and the various individual monthly advertising outlays cannot be analyzed. The "longest" regression that was run with the monthly data tends to indicate that beyond the second preceding month advertising ceases to contribute to variations in sales:

R4.1:

$$S_t = 659 + .32A_t + .33A_{t-1} + .28A_{t-2} + .13A_{t-3} - .04A_{t-4}$$

		(.09)	(.09)	(.09)	(.09)	(.09)
	146	130	117	109	108	108

$$N = 78 \qquad R^2 = .48$$

(*S* and *A* are monthly sales and advertising expenditures, seasonally adjusted, from Table 2. The units are in hundreds of dollars. *N* is sample size. The multiple coefficient of determination, R^2, is unadjusted for degrees of freedom. Figures in parentheses are standard errors of regression coefficients. Shown on the last line are standard deviations of residuals, calculated as if the regression stopped with that particular variable.)

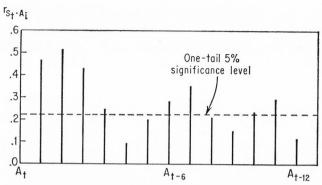

Fig. 4. Simple correlation coefficients of sales on advertising based on monthly data, January 1954–July 1960 ($N = 78$)

There is thus available contradictory evidence of only a very weak nature for and against a definite monthly pattern. It does not permit a strong stand for or against the use of a month as a "true" adjustment period.

This consideration, added to the various previously mentioned grounds, led to the adoption of yearly data as units of observation. However, it should not be overlooked that there were highly practical reasons as well that favored the use of yearly observations. The sample size in the case of monthly data was 636, while there were only 53 annual observations. A thorough testing of the various versions of the Koyck model against other regression models required over 300 separate multiple regression estimates. Even with the help of a computer, considerable effort was spared by not using the monthly data.

Nevertheless, it is of interest to make a brief comparison of the results arrived at by using monthly data (1954–1960) and yearly data. Therefore, the "best" least squares estimate, based on monthly data, of the Koyck model is given here, and it can be compared with the results, based on yearly data, which are given in the following chapter:[1]

R4.2:

$$S_t = 396 + .39\,S_{t-1} + .27\,A_t + .21\,A_{t-1} + .16\,A_{t-2}$$

$$ (.10) \qquad (.08) \qquad (.08) \qquad (.09)$$

$$146 \qquad 113 \qquad\quad 104 \qquad\quad 101 \qquad\quad 99$$

$$N = 78 \qquad R^2 = .56 \qquad d = 2.1$$

---

[1] "Best" estimate in the sense that more than three advertising monthly variables were also used, but beyond A_{t-2} they did not lower the standard deviation of regression residuals.

(d, the Durbin–Watson statistic, at 2.1 suggests little auto-correlation among the residuals.)

The "traditional" model estimates are shown in R4.3 (which benefits from regression's R4.1 demonstration that beyond A_{t-2} no reduction in the standard deviation of the residuals is achieved):

R4.3:

$$S_t = 699 + .32A_t + .33A_{t-1} + .30A_{t-2}$$

$$\begin{array}{cccc} & (.08) & (.09) & (.09) \\ 146 & 130 & 117 & 109 \end{array}$$

$$N = 78 \qquad R^2 = .47$$

(There are 47 runs up and down in the residuals, giving a standard normal variable of approximately minus 3.5. It is evident that there is auto-correlation present.)

It is now necessary to consider variables that may have influenced Pinkham's sales and to decide which of them should be included in the multiple regression analysis. Price appears to have had a relatively minor influence upon the sales of the vegetable compound to the trade. A first, and somewhat crude indication of this is its extraordinary stability. As can be seen from Table 3, only four changes were made in the price of the liquid tonic over almost sixty years, while advertising was subject to constant experimentation.

Referring to this table and to Table 1, the following remarks about the price changes can be made:

(a) Between 1917 and 1918 the price of the liquid tonic increased by almost 24 per cent while sales, rising since 1916, grew from $1,330,000 to $1,980,000 or by about 50 per cent.

(b) While price went up by 11 per cent from 1929 to 1930, sales, diminishing during the four previous years, fell another 4 per cent.

(c) During 1947, the average prevailing price of $10.67[1] was about 7 per cent higher than in 1946 and sales, declining since 1945, shrank by another 12 per cent.

(d) The last price change of the liquid tonic in 1948 was an increase of 12 per cent over the previous year: sales fell by less than one-half of a per cent.

---

[1] From January to May, 1947 the price stood at $10.00. It was then raised to $11.00.

TABLE 3. PRICES TO THE TRADE OF THE VEGETABLE COMPOUND PER DOZEN BOTTLES[a]
1908–1960

Period	Liquid Tonic	Tablets
1905–1917	$7.28	$7.28
1918–1929	9.00	9.00
1930–1946	10.00	10.00
May 1947–December 1947	11.00	no change
January 1948–May 1949	12.00	no change
June 1949–February 1956	no change	9.67
March 1956–October 1956	no change	10.30
November 1956–December 1960	no change	11.00

[a] A standard bottle of the liquid tonic contains $14\frac{1}{2}$ fluid ounces. Within active memory the standard bottle (formerly box) contained 72 tablets.
Source: Company records.

No clear-cut influence of factory price on sales is discernible from these historical episodes. The lack of variability in price precludes correlating it with sales by the method of least squares. Even such measures of association as tetrachoric correlation and non-parametric corner association cannot be usefully employed here because of the lack of change in the exogenous variable.

A more fundamental problem is raised by the nature of the relationship between the factory and the retail price of the vegetable compound. While price to distributors is the relevant price in the analysis of the company's sales variations, it could be normally expected that it is but a faithful reflection of the retail price. This is so because demand on the wholesale level is typically envisaged as being a derived demand. However, if, wholesale price movements are in no way systematically related to changes in the retail price, attention should be shifted to prices at retail level. It appears that such unusual circumstances, in which prices at retail moved independently of prices at wholesale, prevailed over long stretches of the company's history. Therefore retail price, rather than wholesale price, should be used as an independent variable in the study. Unfortunately this is not possible because retail prices are not known.

Throughout most of the period under review (1908–1960) distributors complained that margins were unsatisfactory and that the vegetable compound was a favorite loss leader. Apparently Lydia Pinkham Company was one of the most unpopular suppliers of the drug wholesale houses. In 1939, under their prodding to "go fair-trade," the company undertook a survey of prices charged to consumers by soliciting the return of package-insert questionnaires.

At the time the survey was taken, a bottle of tonic sold for $.833 CIF (i.e., cost, insurance, freight). Table 4 rather forcibly demonstrates both the loss-leader aspect and the wide range of retail prices of the compound. A similar survey, undertaken between January and March 1947 when the factory price still stood at $.833 a bottle, showed that in 19 states at least 25 per cent of all sales transactions occurred at a price of less than 97 cents. In Arkansas and North Dakota, however, 42 per cent of sales were realized at retail prices exceeding $1.35.

TABLE 4. RETAIL SELLING PRICE OF VEGETABLE COMPOUND FOR 1939[a]
(based on returns of 44,521 questionnaires)

Retail Price Range	Per Cent of Sales Transactions
$ .59–$ .81	6.2
.82– .89	28.3
.90– .96	6.9
.97– 1.00	38.8
1.01– 1.08	3.2
1.09– 1.19	12.3
$1.20–and up	4.3
	100.0

[a] Adapted from Neil H. Borden and Martin V. Marshall, *Advertising Management* (Homewood, Ill.: Richard D. Irwin, Inc., 1959), p. 189.

When the company, as already mentioned in the previous chapter, finally did adopt fair trade in 1948, a retail price of $1.39 was set as the minimum in all states except in the District of Columbia, Missouri, Texas and Vermont, which did not have fair trade laws. In the summer of that year, when the fair trade coverage was not yet complete, another questionnaire survey on retail prices paid was launched. Table 5 summarizes some of the results. The survey did not disclose any systematic differences in retail prices paid between fair-trade and non-fair trade areas.

All the above survey data, and the historical tendency of the retailers to use Lydia Pinkham as a promotional item are taken as evidence of the relatively limited influence of the wholesale price upon the sales of the company—except insofar as it sets a broad floor to the retail price. They are also taken as evidence of the almost insurmountable difficulty, even after the adoption of fair trading, of determining a

TABLE 5. SELECTED DATA ON RETAIL SALES PRICES OF THE LIQUID VEGETABLE COMPOUND DURING THE SUMMER OF 1948

States	Total Number of Sales	Percentage of sales transacted at $1.39 or more
Maine[a]	31	81
North Dakota	5	80
Missouri	69	76
Massachusetts[a]	66	74
Arkansas	82	73
.	.	.
.	.	.
.	.	.
New Mexico	23	61
New Hampshire[a]	19	58
Missouri	108	52
.	.	.
.	.	.
.	.	.
Louisiana	76	51
North Carolina[a]	62	50
Wyoming	6	50
.	.	.
.	.	.
.	.	.
South Carolina	85	35
Connecticut[a]	12	33
Wisconsin	69	32
Virginia[a]	106	31
Ohio	199	29
.	.	.
.	.	.
.	.	.
Pennsylvania	223	15
Rhode Island[a]	11	9
New Jersey	75	2

[a] States in which minimum retail price was in effect.
Source: Company records.

representative price at retail. It might also be reasonably conjectured that as the medicine has no very close rivals, the substitution price effect would be weak. The decision was therefore taken not to include the price of the vegetable compound among the variables to be used in the multiple regression analysis.

It seems plausible to speculate that, in the economists' language, the vegetable compound is an inferior good. As the consumer's disposable income increases, she is likely, if suffering real discomfort, to rely more and more on her physician for advice that she can now afford. And the physicians, as company officials pointed out, do not particularly care for prescribing proprietary medicines. Yet this really is speculation. In general, self-medication has not been known to decrease in our prosperous times.

Figure 5, based on Tables 1 and 6, shows sales and disposable personal income plotted over time. No clear relationship between the two variables is discernible. Non-parametric tests of dependence among them were inconclusive. It was finally decided, after much computational work had already been done, to include disposable personal income among the independent variables used in the regression analysis.

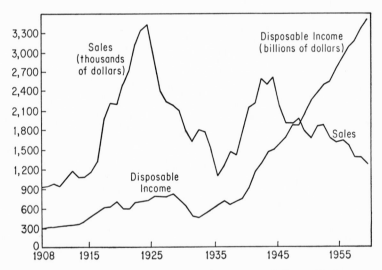

Fig. 5. Sales of Lydia Pinkham Company and disposable income, 1908–1960

Disposable income is regarded here as a proxy for the medical care a consumer can afford. Attention to indicators more closely connected with health care failed, however, to disclose one that would be helpful in explaining movements in the sales of the vegetable compound.

TABLE 6. DISPOSABLE PERSONAL INCOME, 1908–1961
(in billions of current dollars)

Year	Income	Year	Income
1908	29.5[a]	1935	58.3
09	30.2[b]	36	66.2
		37	71.0
1910	30.5	38	65.7
11	31.9	39	70.4
12	33.9		
13	34.8	1940	76.1
14	35.8	41	93.0
15	40.2	42	117.5
16	47.8	43	133.5
17	55.2	44	146.8
18	62.3	45	150.4
19	63.3[c]	46	160.6
		47	170.1
1920	71.5	48	189.3
21	60.2	49	189.7
22	60.3		
23	69.7	1950	207.7
24	71.4	51	227.5
25	73.0	52	238.7
26	77.4	53	252.5
27	77.4	54	256.9
28	77.5	55	274.4
29	83.1	56	292.9[d]
		57	308.8
1930	74.4	58	317.9
31	63.8	59	337.3
32	48.7		
33	45.7	1960	351.8
34	52.0	61	364.9[e]

[a] Extrapolated from Nerlove-Waugh data.

[b] 1909–1918 figures from Nerlove and Waugh, *op. cit.*, pp. 813–37, Table 1.

[c] 1919–1955 figures from U.S. Bureau of the Census, *Historical Statistics of the United States, Colonial Times to 1957* (Washington, D. C., 1960).

[d] 1956–1960 figures from U.S. Department of Commerce, Office of Business Economics, *Survey of Current Business* (July, 1961), Table 4, p. 8.

[e] *Survey of Current Business* (May, 1962), Table 2, p. 7.

Thus, for instance, there does not seem to be any significant interdependence between consumer expenditures on medical care and Pinkham sales. Estimates of health care expenditures are available on an annual basis only since 1929 and they are given in Table 7. When

Pinkham sales are plotted against them, as in Fig. 6, the corner test of association does not indicate any correlation between the two variables.[1]

Thought has also been given to a possible connection between epidemics and upward movements of sales, even though this would contribute explanation of an episodic character only. The phenomenal spurt of Lydia Pinkham's sales started in 1917 and reached its peak in 1925. The beginning coincides with, but the peak postdates by several years, the Spanish flu epidemic in the United States. Another epidemic, encephalitis lethargica, a virus infection having as its consequence

TABLE 7. EXPENDITURES ON MEDICAL CARE, 1929–1960
(in billions of dollars)

Year	Expenditure	Year	Expenditure
1929	2.9[a]	1945	5.0
		46	6.1[b]
1930	2.8	47	6.8
31	2.5	48	7.7
32	2.1	49	8.2
33	2.0		
34	2.2	1950	8.7
35	2.3	51	9.4
36	2.5	52	10.2
37	2.7	53	11.1
38	2.7	54	11.9
39	2.8	55	12.8
		56	14.1[c]
1940	3.0	57	15.4
41	3.3	58	16.6
42	3.7	59	18.2
43	4.2		
44	4.7	1960	19.7

[a] 1929–1945 figures from U.S. Department of Commerce, Office of Business Economics, *National Income (1954) Edition* (Washington, D.C., 1954), Table 30, pp. 206–207, lines 42–50.

[b] 1946–1955 figures from U.S., D.C., O.B.E., *U.S. Income and Output* (Washington, D.C., November, 1958), Table II–4, p. 150.

[c] U.S., D.C., O.B.E., *Survey of Current Business* (July, 1961), Table II–4, p. 14.

---

[1] If the number of physicians per 100,000 of population is taken as an index of the medical care available to the public, it could be expected that there would be an inverse relationship between it and Pinkham sales. The average number of physicians (based on biennial estimates) during the decade 1910–20 was 143.4; during 1920–30, 128.5; during 1930–40, 127.8; during 1940–50, 134 and during the last decade it was 132.6 (U.S. Bureau of the Census, *Historical Statistics of the United States, Colonial Times to 1957* (Washington D.C., 1960), Table B. 18, p. 34. The index thus seems to have been remarkably stable and apparently not related to Pinkham sales.

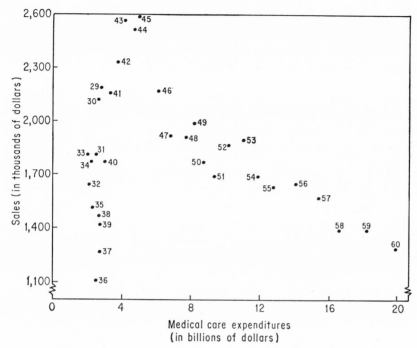

Fig. 6. Sales of Lydia Pinkham Company plotted against expenditures on medical care, 1929–1960

Parkinson's disease, reached American shores in 1917 and practically disappeared in 1925. However, any thought about the liquid tonic being used as a preventive "folk" medicine had to be discarded, when it was realized that this much investigated epidemic counted its American victims in tens, or, at most, hundreds a year only.[1]

It has been suggested, only half jokingly, that the liquid tonic may have served as a substitute for conventional alcoholic beverages. Throughout most of the period under review the compound's volumetric alcohol content stood at 15 per cent, a strength comparable to that of Marsala or port wines. The thought of Lydia Pinkham's medicine serving as a respectable woman's apéritif in puritanical or fundamentalist regions cannot be dismissed off-hand. Also, in times of shortages or restrictions of alcoholic drinks, such as the Prohibition Era, thirsty customers have been known to turn to even less orthodox drinks.

---

[1] Third Report of the Matheson Committee, *Epidemic Encephalitis* (New York: Columbia University Press, 1939).

The bitter and strong taste of the medicine is *prima facie* evidence against the idea of substitution, unless one entertains the more sophisticated thought of masochism contributing to greater drinking enjoyment. An informal experiment conducted about twenty-five years ago on a few alcoholics in the Lynn municipal jail showed that even these veteran practitioners could not absorb more than a fourteen ounce bottle before their stomachs turned. The growing share of tablets in the total sales of the company—in 1956 almost half the dollar sales were accounted for by tablets—renders the thought of substitutability even more tenuous.

Statistical evidence on this issue could be obtained, in principle, by looking for a (negative) association between sales of the *liquid* compound and United States alcoholic beverage consumption figures. Unfortunately, estimates of sales of the liquid tonic are not available for most of the period. Estimates of national consumption of alcoholic beverages are so unreliable for the period 1919 to 1935 that no faith can be placed in them.[1]

Over the period considered, changes in the product were not drastic and were not followed by any wide swings in sales. This is the summary of the scattered references to them in the previous chapter: in 1914 the solid herbal content was increased sevenfold; in 1916 alcohol content was reduced from about 18 to 15 per cent by volume; in 1937 Vitamin B1 was added to the tonic and ferrous sulphate to the tablets; in 1951 Jamaica dogwood was in part substituted for true and false unicorn in the formula; in 1952 alcohol content was further reduced to 13.5 per cent and the package was slightly changed.

Although the evidence is scanty, the composition of Lydia Pinkham's customers seems to have remained about the same over time. According to company records there were 1,400 buyers in 1946. Drug wholesalers accounted for 62 per cent of total sales volume, drug chains took 25 per cent and retailers and others (druggists, food stores) and mail order houses purchased the remaining 13 per cent. In 1958 there were 1,100 customers. Wholesale druggists bought 71 per cent of the total sales volume in that year, drug chains 21 per cent and the remaining 8 per cent was divided among drug and food retailers, department stores, rack jobbers, and mail order houses.

Since it appeared that neither product change nor the composition of marketing channels influenced sales very much, both these variables were dropped from further consideration.

---

[1] Estimates of alcohol consumption for the period 1908 to 1960, as well as an explanation of how they were obtained, are given in the Appendix.

In the last decade of the nineteenth and well into the present century the absolute advertising expenditures incurred by Lydia Pinkham were sufficient to make it a relatively important advertiser on the national scene, particularly in newspapers. Since the nineteen twenties, however, and particularly since the last war, the total volume of national and local advertising has increased so much that it is in order to consider whether Pinkham's sales were not affected by the growing clamor of advertisers for the consumer's attention. This should not be interpreted as implying that Pinkham's advertising dollar does not now buy as much consumer exposure as in the Compound's heroic age (the point was made on page 30). Rather, it may be that the increasing advertising "noise" blunts the consumer's power of absorption of messages.

The meager evidence available does not bear this idea out. *Printer's Ink* estimates of the total national and local advertising volume were obtained for the years 1904, 1909 and 1914, and for all subsequent years until and including 1959 (see Table 8). The arithmetic average of the values for the years 1904, 1909 and 1914 ($1,088 million) was taken as the base of an advertising volume index computed for the years 1914 to 1959. Incidentally, in that latter year the index reached 1,000, ten times the value of 1914 and almost nine times the value of 1933.

When estimates of yearly advertising volume are plotted against sales and divided by medial lines (lines drawn through the sample median observation), a coefficient of medial correlation can be calculated.[1] Its value was obtained. At plus .22 it cannot be considered significant at the 5 per cent level by conventional standards. However, it is interesting to note that what "gross" association there is, appears to be positive rather than negative, as was expected.

For a long time most of Lydia Pinkham's advertising budget was spent on newspaper advertising, with testimonials dominating the copy. Some space was also bought in women's magazines. Between 10 and 15 per cent of advertising outlays were spent on so-called general advertising, mostly informative booklets about feminine hygiene and small premiums, such as sewing kits, given in reward for returning filled in consumer questionnaires. This pattern persisted until the time of the court decision in 1937, when, for the first time, heavy use was made of radio. After more than a year of a national network program the com-

---

[1] Coefficient of medical correlation

$$= \frac{2(\text{total number of points in northeast and southwest quadrants})}{N} - 1$$

See M. H. Quenouille, *Associated Measurements* (New York: Academic Press, 1952), p. 45 and Appendix Table 25.

TABLE 8. ESTIMATED U.S. ADVERTISING VOLUME, 1914–1959
(IN MILLIONS OF DOLLARS AND INDEX FORM)[a]

Year	Million of Dollars	Volume Index[b]
1904	821	
1909	1,142	
1914	1,302	
1915	1,302	119.7
16	1,468	134.9
17	1,627	149.5
18	1,468	134.9
19	2,282	209.7
1920	2,935	269.8
21	2,282	209.7
22	2,607	239.6
23	2,935	269.8
24	2,935	269.8
25	3,099	284.8
26	3,262	299.8
27	3,262	299.8
28	3,262 [sic]	299.8
29	3,426	314.9
1930	2,607	239.6
31	2,282	209.7
32	1,627	149.5
33	1,302	119.7
34	1,627	149.5
35	1,690	155.3
36	1,902	174.8
37	2,071	190.3
38	1,904	175.0
39	1,980	182.0
1940	2,088	191.9
41	2,236	205.5
42	2,156	198.2
43	2,496	229.4
44	2,724	250.4
45	2,874	264.2
46	3,364	309.2
47	4,260	391.5
48	4,864	447.1
49	5,202	478.1
1950	5,710	524.8
51	6,426	590.6
52	7,156	657.7
53	7,755	712.8
54	8,164	750.4
55	9,194	845.0
56	9,904	910.3
57	10,311	947.7
58	10,302	946.9
59	11,117	1,021.8

[a] The dollar figures are taken from U.S. Bureau of the Census, *Historical Statistics, op. cit.*, p. 526, with the exception of the years 1958 and 1959. These were obtained from *Printer's Ink* (September 9, 1960), pp. 340–41.

[b] The arithmetic mean ($1,088,000) of advertising expenditures in the years 1904, 1909 and 1914 was taken as the base (i.e., 100) of the advertising volume index. Before 1914 only quinquennial estimates are available.

pany started using spot radio announcements and did not return to sponsorship of a national broadcast.

From then on there was constant switching of emphasis from newspapers to spot radio, with a steady trickle of outlays on magazine space. In the years 1955 to 1957 there were large-scale experiments with television spot announcements and this medium was subsequently not used. Postwar management and agency thinking on media can be summarized by saying that the traditionally "local" character of Pinkham's advertising is best served by switching systematically from local newspaper ads to radio spot announcements, and that some money ought always to be spent on magazine space, pamphlets and experimentation with new media possibilities. Approximate percentage allocations of the advertising budget for selected years are shown in Table 9.

TABLE 9. PERCENTAGES OF PINKHAM'S ADVERTISING BUDGET IN VARIOUS MEDIA DURING SELECTED YEARS

Year	Newspapers	Magazines	General Advertising[a]	Radio	TV
1914	78	b	22	..	..
1925	80	b	20	..	..
1933	78	b	22	..	..
1938	44	b	10	46	..
1945	83	13	4	..	..
1952	57	3	3	37	..
1956	63	6	3	14	14
1959	80	c	3	17	..

[a] General advertising comprises pamphlets, premiums for answers to questionnaires enclosed in packages and, until 1938, charges for the department replying to customer inquiries.

[b] Cost of magazine advertising included in newspaper advertising.

[c] Less than 1 per cent.

Source: Company records.

Reliance on one as against another medium does not seem to have brought about important changes in sales. The pattern of media use was both simple and stable until the nineteen thirties while there were great fluctuations in sales; from 1937 on there was yearly switching from newspapers to radio and even to television, but sales persisted in their upward or downward movements without regard to these quite drastic changes in media use. Since, in addition, no historical episode seems to point to an important change in the media mix being followed by an important change in sales, it was decided not to include the media mix as an independent variable for regression analysis.

The surprising downturn of sales in 1926 is just that sort of historical incident which led to the consideration of copy "quality" as a possible exogenous variable influencing sales. The main purpose of this chapter was to clear the way for the subsequent testing of the cumulative effects model and the greatest part of it consisted of consideration of a host of variables, other than advertising expenditure, that might have affected Pinkham's sales, and to retain or eliminate them. All of them, except personal disposable income, were eliminated with greater or lesser conviction but copy "quality" is retained for regression analysis. It will be recalled that the Food and Drug Administration moved twice, in 1914 and in 1925, to restrict copy claims. Its successor in watchdog duties over drug advertising copy, the Federal Trade Commission, after a two-year quarrel, allowed the company in 1940 to strengthen its copy again. There are three turning points in the character of the claims and appeals that were used to advertise the compound. Before 1914 the tonic was advertised as a medicine for everything from "female troubles" to cancer of the womb. From the summer of 1914 until December, 1925, the copy concentrated mainly on its powers to relieve menstrual pains, symptoms of menopause and to act as a general tonic. From then until 1940 basically nothing else but claims of tonic action could be put forward on behalf of the vegetable compound. From about the middle of 1940 Pinkham's advertising agency started anticipating FTC's stipulation, which came in December, 1940 and allowed the company again to advertise the effectiveness of the vegetable compound against dysmenorrhea (menstrual pain) and menopausal complaints.

Consider now the evolution of sales at these turning points. Sales were rising in 1912 and 1913, declined in 1914 and did not change in 1915, before starting to move up in 1916. An almost uninterrupted (one exception in 1920) eleven years' increase of sales came to an abrupt halt in 1926. During 1939 sales declined, increased considerably in 1940 and rose a good deal in 1941. The evidence seems most convincing for the 1925–26 change. Reduction in copy strength was more drastic than in 1914 and the downturn in sales pronounced. Furthermore, no other explanation for this downturn can be suggested.

"Copy" was therefore accepted as an exogenous variable for regression analysis. The next chapter explains how this "qualitative" variable was assigned quantitative values and considers the advantages of incorporating "trend" as part of the analysis.

CHAPTER 5

The Results

This chapter presents an evaluation of the cumulative effects model as applied to the Pinkham data. The chief method of evaluating the model is least squares multiple regression analysis.

In the previous chapter the choice was made of the independent variables to be used in explaining variations in the sales revenue of Lydia Pinkham Company. In addition to the lagged sales revenue which Koyck's model requires, advertising expenditures and copy "quality" were settled upon. A variable representing trend will also be included on occasion.

Since the changes in the character of the copy were of a qualitative nature and could not be translated into numbers, copy was taken to be a dummy variable having the values of either 0 or 1 (analogous to a state of "off" and "on"). Such a dummy can be viewed as a shift variable that changes the intercept of the regression hyperplane, but not its slope. Three dummies were used to represent copy: $D1$ was assigned the value of 1 from 1908 to 1914 and of 0 thereafter. $D2$ was given 0 from 1908 to 1914, a value of 1 from 1915 to 1925, and of 0 thereafter. The third dummy, $D3$, was assigned a value of 0 from 1908 to 1925, a value of 1 from 1926 to 1940, and a value of 0 for the rest of the period. In this way each of the four periods of broadly similar copy is represented.

A thorough way of evaluating an econometric model requires that it be judged by several criteria which are not always in complete harmony. Moreover, the model's performance should also be judged against that of alternative models, applied to the same set of data.

While there is no set of rules for picking and choosing among several plausible models, it is commonly agreed that certain things can reasonably be expected of a "good" model. Ferber and Verdoorn suggest some areas that should be considered when appraising a model:

1. The extent of agreement of the (model) estimates with a priori notions of the values of the parameters has to be examined . . . . Thus, if a price elasticity of demand comes out positive . . . the model might well need reworking . . . .

2. The implications of the results have to be assessed, particularly in the light of such other information about the signs and magnitudes of the parameters as may be available . . . .

3. The ability of the model to explain fluctuations in the endogenous variable during the period of observation needs study . . . the focus of such a study is on the detection of systematic patterns in the residuals . . . .

4. The acid test of the model is its predictive ability. The fact that a model survives all other tests with flying colors does not mean it will yield reliable predictions . . . .[1]

The first two sets of considerations could be labeled somewhat loosely as economic criteria. They will be applied to the fullest possible extent to the results. The last two might be labeled statistical criteria. It is among these that conflict may often be found.

The ability of the model to *explain* fluctuations in the dependent variable (for the sample for which computations are made) is called in regression analysis "goodness of fit." There are several indicators of the quality of the fit of a regression equation (which embodies the model) to the data: standard deviation of the regression residuals, coefficient of determination (R^2), ratios of the estimates of the regression coefficients to their standard errors, correlations to determine the extent of intercorrelation between the independent variables. As was stressed in the above quotation the most important of them, however, is an indication of the absence or presence of autocorrelation in the residuals of the regression. If the existence of autocorrelation is detected, it means that certain regularities are still present in the unexplained variance, and hence that the model is not correctly specified.[2]

With the exception of the standard deviation of the residuals, which enters into the formula of the standard error of the forecast, none of

---

[1] R. Ferber and P. J. Verdoorn, *Research Methods in Economics and Business* (New York: The Macmillan Company, 1962), pp. 424–25.

[2] For a lucid discussion of this subject see *ibid.*, pp. 100–101.

these correlation measures of fit is linked directly to that other fundamental statistical criterion by which econometric models are judged—predictive ability. Indeed, an example can be given in which the "violation" of the most important condition of fit may be of benefit to the forecaster. Frequently there is strong autocorrelation among residuals, but the analyst is hard put to find the missing variable which is the culprit. As a consequence, a good explanation, description, fit cannot be achieved. The underlying data-generating mechanism remains veiled to the observer. But if interest centers on *prediction*, attention is diverted from the estimates of the parameters to the forecast. The autoregressivity is accepted, even though it is not explained, and built explicitly into the model.[1] Almost certainly the forecasts of a regression equation are thereby improved, even if the understanding of the mechanism of the regression remains unsatisfactory.

There is a powerful school of thought which puts much emphasis on the predictive ability of the model, almost to the exclusion of considerations relating to explanation or fit. Among economists a leading exponent of this school is Friedman, who would—to put it in an oversimplified manner—rather have a theory which does not seem to be descriptively realistic, but whose predictions are good, than the other way around.[2] For many purposes this is an attractive position. But often the forces of circumstance prevent the analyst from adopting it completely. How is he to decide between two models if the estimates of one give a better fit to the data while the forecast of the other is closer to the actual outcome—but there is only *one* forecasting period available for verification? On this issue Theil states:

> . . . almost always the number of observations is limited, and part of them have to be used to specify the model itself. The temptation is then great to use all or most of the observations for this purpose, so that the possibility of testing the model by means of observations outside the sample used is considerably reduced. The econometrician is then forced to retreat from the prediction criterion, and he can do no more than choose his model in such a way as to maximize the chance that it predicts well.[3]

---

[1] J. Johnston, *Econometric Methods* (New York: McGraw-Hill, Inc., 1963), p. 194.

[2] Milton Friedman, *Essays in Positive Economics* (Chicago: University of Chicago Press, 1953).

[3] H. Theil, *Economic Forecasts and Policy*, 2d ed. rev. (Amsterdam: North-Holland Publishing Co., 1961), p. 205.

However, sometimes fortune smiles upon the investigator and one model gives a better fit as well as a better forecast than the others. Nonetheless, the considerations discussed above must be kept in mind as the evaluation of the models gets underway.

It will be recalled that the simplest version of the cumulative effects model in the present case is

$$(5.1a) \qquad\qquad S_t = k + \alpha A_t + \lambda S_{t-1} \qquad\qquad (KOYK)$$

A slight difference is introduced if the advertising variable is used in logarithmic form to express a belief that there are decreasing returns to advertising:

$$(5.1b) \qquad\qquad S_t = k + \alpha \log A_t + \lambda S_{t-1} \qquad\qquad (KOYL)$$

Three alternatives to Koyck's model were subjected to least squares regression. They appear below in their simplest versions:

$$(5.2a, b) \quad S_t = k + \beta A_t \quad (NOYK) \qquad S_t = k + \beta \log A_t \quad (NOYL)$$

(5.2), in its simple or semilogarithmic form, can perhaps be called the traditional model for the regression measurement of advertising effectiveness.

$$(5.3) \qquad\qquad \Delta S_t = k + \beta \Delta A_t \qquad\qquad (DIF)$$

This model uses first differences instead of the original data and despite its simplicity can be considered a more attractive way of attacking the measurement problem than (5.2). If there is some positive serial correlation in the data, as is usually the case with economic time series, recourse to first differences will tend to reduce it. Though not, as Telser has shown, necessarily inconsistent with the cumulative effects model, the first difference model can be considered as the most important challenger of it.[1]

Finally, equation (5.4) in various versions was also fitted by least squares.

$$(5.4) \qquad\qquad \Delta \log S_t = k + \beta \Delta \log A_t \qquad\qquad (LOF)$$

It is simply a logarithmic form of (5.3) and its drawback is that the standard error of its estimate cannot be compared to those of the other models which are directly and immediately comparable.[2]

---

[1] Lester G. Telser, "Advertising and Cigarettes," *Journal of Political Economy,* **LXX** (October, 1962), 471–99.

[2] As a matter of fact, the intention was to use only the advertising variable in logarithmic form, but through a mistake the sales variable was converted into logarithms as well and the calculations were finished before the error was discovered.

The very large number of regression estimates makes it necessary to adopt a procedure of step-by-step elimination of uninteresting results.[1] Such a procedure was built around the four basic models (5.1) to (5.4). It will be convenient to give these models code names before proceeding any further. (5.1a) is called KOYK, while (5.1b) is given the name of KOYL (the L standing for logarithm). Analogously (5.2a) and (5.2b) are designated as NOYK and NOYL, respectively ("not Koyck"). The first difference model (5.3) is called DIF and (5.4), the model with first differences of logarithms, has the name of LOF.

Equations (5.1) to (5.4) show only the simplest version of these models. It was mentioned that five more variables are to be included— the three dummies standing for copy, disposable income and, on occasion, trend. Consideration had also to be given to the possibility that the postulated reaction in the cumulative effects model does not start immediately, but only after one or two periods. This required the inclusion of at least the last, and the one but last, year's advertising expenditures, A_{t-1} and A_{t-2}. To give the other models the same "chance," NOYK's and NOYL's were also estimated with A_{t-1} and A_{t-2}. The first difference models (DIF's and LOF's) were estimated with up to four preceding years of advertising expenditure, that is with A_{t-1} to A_{t-4}.

To see if the results of the regressions covering the whole period 1908–1960 were consistent with results for shorter periods, regressions were run on all model versions for the sub-periods 1908–1940, 1908–1934 and 1926–1960. These sub-periods will be called A, B and C, respectively. For some model versions the sub-periods 1908–1925, 1915–1934, 1935–1960 and 1941–1960 were also covered.[2]

The intention is to select one or several "best" regressions of each basic model and enter these into the "finals" for comparison and thorough evaluation. All those model versions that have one or more lagged advertising variables will first be considered with elimination in mind. They are set out in a simplified form in Table 10.

Neither the KOYL nor the KOYK forms of the cumulative effects model appear to give useful results when one or two lagged advertising

---

[1] At this point reference is made to the Preface in which a brief account was given of the computational work connected with this dissertation.

[2] These sub-periods were chosen because 1914, 1925 and 1940 are the years of copy change. 1934–1935 is the time when the drastic curtailment of advertising expenditures invites a forecasting test of the estimates.

TABLE 10. SIMPLIFIED SUMMARY OF REGRESSIONS WITH ONE OR MORE LAGGED
VARIABLES THAT WERE ELIMINATED

KOYK	$S_t = S_{t-1} + (\log)A_t + (\log)A_{t-1} + (\log)A_{t-2}$
or KOYL	$= S_{t-1} + (\log)A_t + (\log)A_{t-1}$
NOYK	$S_t = (\log)A_t + (\log)A_{t-1} + (\log)A_{t-2}$
or NOYL	$= (\log)A_t + (\log)A_{t-1}$
DIF	$\Delta(\log)S_t = \Delta(\log)A_t + \Delta(\log)A_{t-1} + \Delta(\log)A_{t-2} + \Delta(\log)A_{t-3} + \Delta(\log)A_{t-4}$
or	$= \Delta(\log)A_t + \Delta(\log)A_{t-1} + \Delta(\log)A_{t-2} + \Delta(\log)A_{t-3}$
LOF	$= \Delta(\log)A_t + \Delta(\log)A_{t-1} + \Delta(\log)A_{t-2}$

Periods: 1908–60
1908–40 (A); 1908–34 (B); 1926–60 (C).

variables are incorporated into them. A typical example is a KOYL
version with three dummies and trend:

$$S_t = -1271 + .79 S_{t-1} + 1298 \log A_t - 487 \log A_{t-1} - 312 \log A_{t-2}$$

$$\begin{array}{ccccc}
& (.10) & (302) & (358) & (287) \\
629 & 233 & 221 & 196 & 185
\end{array}$$

$$+ 135D1 + 291D2 - 29D3 + 4.18T$$

$$\begin{array}{cccc}
(254) & (188) & (115) & (5.57) \\
186 & 176 & 174 & 175
\end{array}$$

$$N = 53 \qquad R^2 = .933$$

(S and A are yearly sales and advertising expenditures in thousands of
dollars. D's stand for dummies which represent the qualities of advertising copy as explained on page 78: $D1$ has the value of 1 from 1908
to 1914 and of 0 thereafter; $D2$ is 0 from 1908 to 1914, 1 from 1915 to
1925 and 0 subsequently; $D3$ is 0 from 1908 to 1925, 1 from 1926 to
1940 and 0 thereafter. T represents trend and was given values from 1
to 53, starting with the year 1908. N is the sample size and R^2 the unadjusted coefficient of multiple determination. Figures in parentheses
are standard errors of the coefficients. Shown on the last line are standard deviations of residuals calculated by the stepwise process as if the
regression had stopped with that particular variable. Unless expressly
mentioned, the regression results will be shown in this manner throughout the chapter.)

Attention is drawn to the negative values of the regression coefficients of the lagged advertising variables and to the unfavorable ratio of these coefficients to their standard errors. Two explanations suggest themselves for the negative signs. The first is that past advertising outlays hinder current sales. This explanation, on a priori economic considerations, makes about as much sense as a positive price elasticity of demand. The second explanation is that the discordant signs are essentially a symptom of the inadequacy of the regression model.

Dropping off, successively, the trend term and the dummies does not change the essential picture: the regression coefficients of the lagged advertising variables keep their negative signs. This is also true when only A_{t-1} is used as a lagged advertising variable.

When the shorter period A (1908–1940) is subjected to regression analysis, the broad picture remains the same as that for the whole period: the regression coefficients of A_{t-2} and A_{t-1} are negative and their standard errors are large.[1] However, trend comes alive both according to conventional tests and as a factor that reduces the standard deviation of the residuals. The periods B (1908–1934) and C (1926–1960) follow the pattern of A: coefficients are negative, errors large and trend is discernible.

The KOYK regressions follow an almost identical path. Regression coefficients are negative and trend seems important, except during the basic period of analysis, 1908–1960.

A similar pattern holds for the NOYK and NOYL regressions that have two or one lagged advertising variables. The partials of those variables are negative and are not significant by conventional standards. Furthermore, the addition of these variables to the regression increases the standard deviation of the residuals. This pattern holds for the sub-periods A, B and C as well. Leaving out, successively, the trend term and the dummies does not improve the situation.

Roughly the same pattern emerges from the least squares estimates of first differences. Through the basic period and sub-periods A, B and C the DIF and LOF forms have very large standard errors of regression coefficients pertaining to A_{t-4}, A_{t-3} and A_{t-2}. These lagged variables, as they are added to the regression also increase the standard deviation of the residuals. When the dummies are dropped the situation remains unchanged. The first difference models with only one lagged advertising

---

[1] Three dummies are used to handle the four different eras of advertising copy claims. When the regression stops at the year 1940, only two are used: $D1$ has the value 1 from 1908 until 1914, zero thereafter. $D2$ is zero until 1914, one until 1925, zero thereafter. In a similar fashion, the sub-periods 1926–1960, 1915–1934, 1935–1960 and 1941–1960 have each only one dummy.

variable behave, however, in a different manner. They will be discussed later.

To sum up the elimination process concerning models incorporating one or more lagged advertising variables: KOYK, KOYL, NOYK and NOYL models with two or one lagged advertising variables (and dummies and a trend variable, or just dummies, or neither) were estimated by least squares for the period 1908 to 1960 and the sub-periods A (1908–40), B (1908–34) and C (1926–60). These 96 regression estimates were eliminated for the reasons outlined above. Eliminated in a similar fashion were 48 regression estimates of the DIF and LOF models incorporating two or more lagged advertising variables (with or without dummies) and covering the same periods.

After eliminating a large number of unusable results (144 regressions), the choice of estimates to be kept for final comparisons must be narrowed down still further. Before discussing the criteria employed in this weeding-out process, it will repay us to pause briefly and take stock of the regression estimates still to be considered. Most of them, like their eliminated companions, were calculated on a Univac I computer. However, a small proportion was calculated later on an IBM 1620 computer and will be referred to as "second-generation" estimates. These estimates will be described in due course. The "first-generation," Univac-calculated regressions that remain for consideration are set out in a simplified form in Table 11.

TABLE 11. SIMPLIFIED SUMMARY OF FIRST GENERATION REGRESSIONS REMAINING AFTER FIRST ROUND OF ELIMINATIONS

KOYK	$S_t = S_{t-1} + (\log)A_t + D1 + D2 + D3 + T$
or	$= S_{t-1} + (\log)A_t + D1 + D2 + D3$
KOYL	$= S_{t-1} + (\log)A_t$
NOYK	$S_t = (\log)A_t + D1 + D2 + D3 + T$
or	$= (\log)A_t + D1 + D2 + D3$
NOYL	$= (\log)A_t$
	$\Delta(\log)S_t = \Delta(\log)A_t + \Delta(\log)A_{t-1} + D1 + D2 + D3$
DIF	$= \Delta(\log)A_t + \Delta(\log)A_{t-1}$
or	$= \Delta(\log)A_t + D1 + D2 + D3$
LOF	$= \Delta(\log)A_t$

Periods: 1908–60
       1908–40 (A); 1908–34 (B); 1926–60 (C).

Several statistical criteria are used in the elimination of further regression estimates. The greatest importance is attached to the standard deviation of the regression residuals (also called the standard error of the estimate) and to estimates of linear independence among successive regression disturbances.

There are several reasons which account for the usefulness of the standard deviation of residuals as a yardstick by which to judge regression results. It enters the formula of the standard error of forecast and is thus the only regression measure related directly to the predictive ability of the regression equation. The standard error of estimate is essentially a measure of the root mean square discrepancy between the observations and the fitted line and in this sense a measure of the goodness of fit, in units in which the dependent variable is measured.[1] Both the Univac and IBM computer programs, which were used, were stepwise regression programs and gave information about the size of the standard error of estimate for each independent variable added to the right-hand side of the equation. Judgment was thus not restricted to comparisons between "final" regression estimates, but could also be formed about the usefulness of individual exogenous variables (i.e., whether their inclusion reduced the variation in the endogenous variable or not).[2]

Lack of independence among successive residuals suggests that variables influencing the dependent factor have been left out of the regression, or that the functional form of the regression was not well chosen. In other words, the model is not correctly specified. A test for

---

[1] The standard error of estimate, however, offers no measure of the *proportion* of the variation in the dependent variable which is associated with the variation in the independent factors. This proportion is measured by the coefficient of multiple determination, R^2. (In Bayesian language, R^2 is a ratio of the variances of the posterior distributions of the dependent variable which do and do not use information in the independent variables.)

Many statisticians frown, nevertheless, upon indiscriminate use of R^2. They point out that the coefficient of determination is a relative measure, depending not only on how well the regression line fits the observations (i.e., on the variance of regression residuals), but also on the amount of the dispersion in the sample observations of the dependent variable (i.e., on their variance). Their position is explained in W. Allen Wallis and Harry V. Roberts, *Statistics—A New Approach* (New York: The Free Press of Glencoe, Inc., 1956), pp. 545–46.

In the present instance, R^2 will continue to be given in order to follow harmless convention.

[2] Such a judgment had to be tempered, however, by the realization that the sequence in which the variables had been added could have influenced the size of the successive standard errors of estimate.

independence among successive regression residuals is based on the
Durbin–Watson statistic, which uses the ratio of the mean-square
successive difference to the variance of residuals. While it underestimates
the extent of autocorrelation among residuals in cases of regressions
where the endogenous variable appears in lagged form among exogenous
variables, it is nevertheless the only test currently available.

On occasion, the ratio of the regression coefficient to its standard
error may be useful in the elimination process. Following accepted
practice, standard errors are listed below the appropriate regression
coefficients.

Looking at the estimates of the various versions of the KOYK
model with one advertising variable, it appears that the following one
represents the "best fit":

KOYK:

$$S_t = 212 + .628\,S_{t-1} + .537\,A_t - 102D1 + 181D2 - 203D3$$

	(.085)	(.143)	(98)	(68)	(70)
629	232	225	226	198	185

$$N = 53 \qquad R^2 = .922 \qquad d = 1.19 \qquad \hat{\rho} = .41$$

(d is the Durbin–Watson statistic. Since

$$d = \frac{\sum\limits_{t=2}^{N} (u_t - u_{t-1})^2}{\sum\limits_{t=1}^{N} u_t^2} \cong 2(1 - \hat{\rho})$$

the estimated coefficient of autocorrelation, $\hat{\rho}$, is approximately .41.)

For the basic period 1908–60 these estimates give the lowest standard error of the KOYK's, lower than with either the trend variable
added or with it and the dummies omitted. Throughout the sub-periods
results that seem reasonable and consistent are obtained, with one
exception: during the periods A, B, 1908–25 and 1914–35 the advertising
variable increases, rather than decreases, the standard error of the
estimate. (In 1926–60, 1935–60, 1941–60 this variable lowers the standard error.) The Durbin–Watson statistic, at 1.19, points to positive
autocorrelation among residuals.

Of the 3 KOYK versions (with T and dummies, without T, and
without T and dummies during 1908–60, 1908–40, 1908–34, 1908–25,
1926–60, 1915–34, 1935–60, 1941–60) only one is thus kept for further
consideration. This is to say that 16 out of the 24 KOYK estimates are
eliminated from further consideration.

As previously stated, the NOYK and NOYL models were fitted by least squares to see how this "traditional" and straightforward way of estimating the effect of advertising measures up to the cumulative effects model. The answer is easily given: not very well.

The choicest of the NOYK's appears thus:

NOYK:

$$S_t = 634 + 1.418A_t - 338D1 + 131D2 - 393D3$$

	(.112)	(124)	(98)	(94)
633	344	329	307	266

$$N = 54 \qquad R^2 = .836$$

(It is to be noted that there are 54 observations in the sample from which the NOYK–NOYL regressions were calculated, or one more than in the KOYK–KOYL regressions which use a lagged variable.) In certain sub-periods, trend improves the performance of this regression slightly. A glance at the standard deviation of regression residuals shows how much this estimate lags behind the chosen KOYK regression in which it is only $185,000.

Even the best of NOYL's does not give a much better fit:

NOYL:

$$S_t = -7280 + 3120 \log A_t - 220D1 + 225D2 - 281D3$$

	(260)	(134)	(101)	(96)
633	331	327	297	277

$$N = 54 \qquad R^2 = .823 \qquad d = 1.04 \qquad \hat\rho = .48$$

The Durbin–Watson statistic was calculated for this regression, where, incidentally, its use is not hamstrung by the presence of a lagged endogenous variable.[1] It indicates moderately strong auto-correlation among the residuals. It was seen that the standard errors were larger in the case of the best NOYK and NOYL models than in the estimates of the best KOYK model. This pattern also holds over all the sub-periods covered. The autocorrelation among residuals in the NOYL choice appeared at least as severe as that in the chosen KOYK. All the other NOYK and NOYL estimates which did not give as good a fit as the two just described were therefore dismissed from future consideration. This eliminated another twenty regression estimates: two models, each with T and dummies and without dummies for the basic period and the sub-periods A, B, C and 1907–1925.

---

[1] Because the calculation of the Durbin–Watson statistic is very time-consuming, it was computed in the most important cases only.

Among the LOF's, the version that seems to perform best incorporates one lagged advertising variable:[1]

LOF:

$$\Delta \log S_t = 5 + 328 \, \Delta \log A_t + 171 \, \Delta \log A_{t-1}$$

$$\begin{array}{ccc} & (86) \ (60) & (60) \\ 58.0 & 47.7 & 44.6 \end{array}$$

$$N = 52 \qquad R^2 = .431 \qquad d = 1.65 \qquad \hat{\rho} = .17$$

When dummies are added to $\Delta \log A_t$ they raise the standard error, but the addition of ΔA_{t-1} lowers such error considerably. Over the sub-periods the results are consistent, but sometimes very weak. Thus for the periods 1909–34, 1909–25 and 1915–34 the coefficient of multiple determination is not significant by conventional statistical standards. The Durbin–Watson statistic indicates very little autocorrelation in the residuals. It is unfortunate that the standard errors of the LOF estimates cannot be compared to those of the other models without much difficulty. The reason for this is that the dependent variable is here expressed in logarithmic form.

Coming now to the two sets of estimates which are the strongest contenders for the title of the best predictor or estimator, the finalist among the first difference models will first be chosen. Of the two, the version with only the current advertising variable and dummies seems, on the whole, superior to the version with one lagged advertising variable and dummies. With the exception of the sub-periods 1926–60, 1908–25 and 1915–34 this version has lower standard errors. The regression estimates for the main periods are given below:

DIF 1:
1908–60

$$\Delta S_t = -16 + .531 \, \Delta A_t + 51D1 + 156D2 - 62D3$$

$$\begin{array}{ccccc} & (124) \ (.119) & (84) & (68) & (62) \\ 236 & 193 & 194 & 182 & 182 \end{array}$$

$$N = 53 \qquad R^2 = .456 \qquad d = 1.78 \qquad \hat{\rho} = .11$$

---

[1] The Univac regression program employed does not accept negative numbers. The observations had therefore to be coded. An error in input instructions omitted the decimal point in the dependent variable. The results of coding can be represented as follows:

$$\Delta \log S_t + 1000 = 506 + 328(\Delta \log A_t + 1) + 171(\Delta \log A_{t-1} + 1)$$

DIF 1.A:
1908–40

$$\Delta S_t = -85 + .431 \, \Delta A_t + 118D1 + 235D2$$

$$\begin{array}{cccc} & (136) & (.135) & (95) & (79) \\ 259 & & 217 & 220 & 197 \end{array}$$

$$N = 33 \qquad R^2 = .478$$

DIF 1.B:
1908–34

$$\Delta S_t = -174 + .352 \, \Delta A_t + 207D1 + 332D2$$

$$\begin{array}{cccc} & (166) & (.159) & (98) & (85) \\ 257 & & 231 & 235 & 186 \end{array}$$

$$N = 27 \qquad R^2 = .536$$

DIF 1.C:
1926–60

$$\Delta S_t = -15 + .597 \, \Delta A_t - 59D$$

$$\begin{array}{ccc} & (126) & (.121) & (60) \\ 229 & & 175 & 175 \end{array}$$

$$N = 35 \qquad R^2 = .451$$

These results are given in some detail so that the reader can more easily visualize the type of work undertaken on most model estimates. These four regressions also show how the marginal effect of advertising on sales was changing within the fifty-three years covered and how, despite these changes, the individual results do not appear to be contradictory. The periods in which heavy advertising expenditure (over, say, $1,200,000 annually) is *relatively* frequent—A and B—show a lower return on the advertising dollar than the other two periods and this seems reasonable if the idea of decreasing returns to the scale of advertising is accepted. The Durbin–Watson statistic gives no evidence of autocorrelation among the residuals.

A KOYL model version gave, at first sight, the best fit of the first-generation Univac-computed estimates:

KOYL 1:
1908–60

$$S_t = -2924 + .633 S_{t-1} + 1226 \log A_t - 20D1 + 215D2 - 164D3$$

$$\begin{array}{cccccc} & (.075) & (282) & (93) & (65) & (63) \\ 629 & 232 & 219 & 221 & 188 & 178 \end{array}$$

$$N = 53 \qquad R^2 = .928 \qquad d = 1.27 \qquad \hat{\rho} = .37$$

This KOYL version (a trend variable did not improve matters here) had the lowest standard error of estimate and small standard errors of partial regression coefficients of the important variables. It gave fairly consistent and reasonable results over all the sub-periods as well, even though in 1908–34, 1908–25 and 1914–35 the advertising variable increased the standard deviation of residuals. However, when the Durbin–Watson statistic was computed it showed signs of correlation among residuals.

The fact that the estimated stochastic disturbances are not serially independent indicate that some systematic influence upon the dependent variable may have been omitted in the model version discussed. Another possible explanation of the autocorrelated residuals is incorrect specification of the functional form of the model, provided there are more or less systematic trends in the independent variables.

While regression theory can cope with autoregressivity, it is nevertheless preferable to seek means which would avoid autocorrelation of residuals altogether.[1] One of the oldest means to do this is the transformation of the series to first differences. This assumes that the autoregressive structure of the disturbance is represented by

$$u_t = \rho u_{t-1} + e_t, \qquad \rho = 1$$

where e_t is independent over time. However, when ρ is smaller than one, the first difference transformation will lead to negative autocorrelation in residuals. Theil and Nagar are two of many writers to recommend that ρ be first estimated and, once estimated, that it be used to transform the original series as follows:[2]

$$y_t - \hat{\rho} y_{t-1} = \alpha(1 - \hat{\rho}) + \beta(x_t - \hat{\rho} x_{t-1}) + (u_t - \hat{\rho} u_{t-1}) + e_t$$

Subtracting $\hat{\rho}$ times the regression equation, lagged one year, from the original equation amounts to a modified first difference transformation and should eliminate most of the interdependence among the observed disturbance terms.[3]

---

[1] The subject is too vast to be entered into here. It has been treated at length in chapter II of Herman Wold, *Demand Analysis* (New York: John Wiley & Sons, Inc., 1953).

[2] H. Theil and A. L. Nagar, "Testing the Independence of Regression Disturbances," *Journal of the American Statistical Association*, **LVI** (December, 1961), pp. 793–807.

[3] Arthur S. Goldberger in his article, "Best Linear Unbiased Prediction in the Generalized Linear Regression Model," *Journal of the American Statistical Association*, **LVII** (June, 1962), pp. 369–75, shows that the efficiency of the expected value estimator relative to the best linear unbiased predictor (which uses information about the residuals' estimated autocorrelation coefficient in the manner employed above) is

Variance (best linear unbiased predictor)

$$= \text{Variance (expected value estimator) } (1 - \rho^2).$$

The principal disadvantage of this method in this case is that the estimated α and λ coefficients no longer lend themselves to such straightforward economic interpretations as those in the simple Koyck model. (Also, the autocorrelation may be of a higher than first order.) The following regression embodies the results obtained when the KOYL equation was transformed and estimated on the IBM 1620:[1]

KOYLDIF:

$$S_t - .37 S_{t-1} = -1903 + .527 (S_{t-1} - .37 S_{t-2})$$
$$\qquad 415 \qquad\qquad\qquad (.085)$$

$$+ 1326 \ (\log A_t - .37 \log A_{t-1}) - 41D1 + 165D2 + 108D3$$
$$\quad (276) \qquad\qquad\qquad\qquad\qquad (84) \qquad (60) \qquad (57)$$
$$\qquad\qquad\qquad\qquad\qquad\qquad\qquad\qquad\qquad\qquad\qquad 163$$

$$N = 53 \qquad R^2 = .864 \qquad d = 1.83 \qquad \hat{\rho} = .08$$

The d statistic, according to the Durbin–Watson tables, does not point to any autocorrelation among residuals. The estimated autocorrelation coefficient shrinks to .08 and the standard error of estimate reaches a low of $163,000.

As these calculations were proceeding two other aspects connected with the analysis emerged. First, the dummies $D1$ and $D3$ did not seem, in *most* of the regressions, to perform very well. Therefore, it was decided to drop them and recalculate the estimates wherever possible without them. Only one dummy, separating the years 1908–1925 (assigned a value of 1) and 1926–1960 (assigned a value of 0) was to be employed. This decision represented the opinion, formed on the basis of the numerical results, that only the 1925 intervention of the federal authorities against copy claims of the company was echoed in the subsequent sales of the company. The regressions of the "second generation" with one dummy only were estimated on the IBM calculator.

Second, and at the same time as this matter was being considered, it appeared from the preliminary tests that disposable income may, after all, have been an important variable affecting Pinkham's sales. Thus it was added to the other exogenous variables in the second generation, IBM estimated, series.

Calculations of the second-generation estimates were, however, restricted to KOYK and DIF models in view of the superior performance of these models—and also for reasons of economy.

---

[1] The regression was estimated at a time when the commercially available "canned" IBM program gave only the final standard error of estimate. Subsequent estimates were calculated with the help of a new *stepwise* IBM program.

The DIF 2 regressions represent the second generation of first difference estimates. The addition of disposable income decreased the standard error of estimate by only about $1,500 in the base period. In the sub-periods A and B the program, set without the prior knowledge of the writer to eliminate all variables not considered by the F test to be significant at the 10 per cent level, rejected the income variable. It can thus be surmised that disposable income would not have performed too well in these sub-periods. Disposable income does not, therefore, appear as an exogenous variable in the final, second-generation, DIF estimates.

DIF 2:
1908–60

$$\Delta S_t = 102 + .562\Delta A_t - 144D$$

$$\begin{array}{ccc} & (.117) & (54) \\ 236 & 193 & 182 \end{array}$$

$$N = 53 \qquad R^2 = .405 \qquad d = 1.71 \qquad \hat{\rho} = .14$$

DIF 2.A:
1908–40

$$\Delta S_t = 110 + .457\Delta A_t - 193D$$

$$\begin{array}{ccc} & (.134) & (71) \\ 259 & 217 & 198 \end{array}$$

$$N = 33 \qquad R^2 = .464$$

DIF 2.B:
1908–34

$$\Delta S_t = 114 + .395\Delta A_t - 286D$$

$$\begin{array}{ccc} & (.158) & (79) \\ 257 & 208 & 189 \end{array}$$

$$N = 27 \qquad R^2 = .464$$

(The dummy, D, has the value 1 from 1908 until 1925, 0 from 1926 on. Standard errors of the constant term—which takes on the role of trend in first difference regressions—were not computed by the IBM program. For reasons of economy, period C estimates [1926–60] were not calculated.)

Because these three estimates give as good a fit as the DIF 1 regressions, yet have two variables less, they are to be preferred to the original first difference regressions.

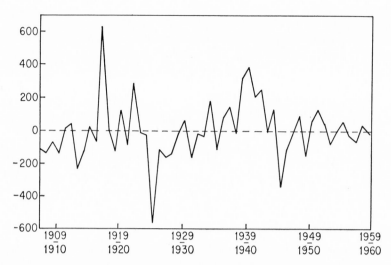

Fig. 7. Residuals from DIF 2 plotted over time

The standard error of estimate of DIF 2 is lower by about $2,500 than that obtained by the best KOYK estimates, which used three more independent variables. The simple correlation coefficient between advertising and the dummy is minus .22, while the highest intercorrelation among independent variables in the chosen KOYK and KOYL models (invariably between S_{t-1} and A_t) reaches .84. The Durbin–Watson statistic does not indicate any autocorrelation among residuals. To give a visual impression of the scatter of residuals, they are plotted over time in Fig. 7. The coefficient of multiple determination is, as is usual in first difference estimates, much lower than in the regressions working with untransformed data. The pattern of the magnitudes of the marginal effect of advertising on sales resembles that shown in the DIF 1 regressions.

When the second-generation KOYL regressions were calculated, disposable personal income did prove to be a variable which gave good results, as can be seen from this best-fitting set of KOYL estimates:

KOYL 2:
1908–60

$$S_t = -3649 + .665\,S_{t-1} + 1180\log A_t + 774D + 32T - 2.83\,Y$$

629 (.063) (243) (107) (5.9) (.67)

232   L 196 178 153

$$N = 53 \qquad R^2 = .941 \qquad d = 1.59 \qquad \hat{\rho} = .20$$

KOYL 2.A:
1908–40

$$S_t = -3793 + .544 S_{t-1} + 1153 \log A_t + 772D + 23T + 7.39Y$$

	(.074)	(224)		(92)	(5.7)	(2.81)
738	255	L		L	142	129

$$N = 33 \qquad R^2 = .969$$

KOYL 2.B:
1908–34

$$S_t = -3575 + .580 S_{t-1} + 1078 \log A_t + 757D + 23T + 6.45Y$$

	(.098)	(455)		(104)	(10)	(3.17)
787	254	L		L	146	136

$$N = 27 \qquad R^2 = .970$$

KOYL 2.C:
1926–60

$$S_t = -3680 + .648 S_{t-1} + 1212 \log A_t + 31T - 2.74Y$$

	(.076)	(253)	(8.4)	(.82)
426	202	173	170	148

$$N = 35 \qquad R^2 = .880$$

(Y is disposable personal income as given in Table 6. The letter L stands for "lowers"—the program employed was one of *stepwise* regression, where variables were ranged from left to right according to their statistical significance by the F test and not necessarily in the sequence presented here. Nevertheless, each of those having an L sign beneath itself did lower the preceding standard error of estimate.)

Of all the regressions computed—on Univac or on IBM—with standard errors of estimate that can be compared, those of the above KOYL 2 series are *the lowest in each of the four periods*. In the base period, the standard error of estimate of KOYL 2 leads the nearest competitor by \$25,000; in sub-period A by \$13,000; in B by \$10,000 and in C by \$10,000.

Also the corresponding ρ estimate at .20 is, following the inclusion of disposable income, considerably lower than either the estimated auto-correlation coefficient of KOYL ($\hat{\rho} = .37$), or the coefficient of the second-generation KOYL regression *without* disposable income:

KOYL 2*Y* less:
1908–60

$$S_t = -3663 + .661 S_{t-1} + 1314 \log A_t + 482D + 9.8T$$

629   (.073)   (280)   (95)   (2.9)

232   *L*   195   178

$$N = 53 \qquad R^2 = .920 \qquad d = 1.16 \qquad \hat{\rho} = .42$$

KOYL 2*Y* less .B:
1908–34

$$S_t = -3243 + .692 S_{t-1} + 997 \log A_t + 757D + 27.4T$$

787   (.087)   (484)   (111)   (10)

254   *L*   *L*   146

$$N = 27 \qquad R^2 = .966$$

KOYL 2*Y* less .C:
1926–60

$$S_t = -2849 + .567 S_{t-1} + 1159 \log A_t + 5T$$

426   (.082)   (290)   (3.4)

203   153   170

$$N = 35 \qquad R^2 = .841$$

The values of the coefficients of advertising once again follow the path first observed in DIF 1—highest in 1926–60, followed by 1908–60 and lowest in 1908–34. The sign of the coefficient of disposable income is not stable—it is negative in the base period and in sub-period C, thus lending support to the inferior good hypothesis, but positive in the other two periods. Figure 8 shows the scatter of KOYL residuals.

The elimination process is now finished. The regression series that seems to *fit* the data best is KOYL 2 and its family. It is pleasant to contemplate the fact that this regression series embodies the cumulative effects model. KOYLDIF, an offshoot of the cumulative effects model, places second in the race, while DIF 2, representing the first difference, non-cumulative approach places third. Table 12 summarizes some of the important information about the "finalists" which represent the "best" version of each model.

Does the KOYL 2 cumulative effects model keep, if not its first, at least a respectable position when required to produce an actual forecast?

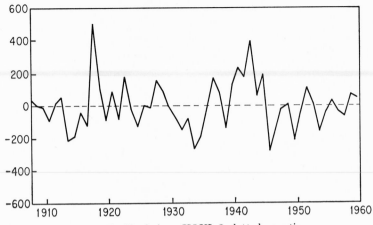

Fig. 8. Residuals from KOYL 2 plotted over time

TABLE 12. STANDARD DEVIATIONS OF RESIDUALS AND ESTIMATED COEFFICIENTS OF
AUTOCORRELATION OF 1908–60 REGRESSONS ADMITTED TO FINALS

Regression Code Name	Standard Deviations of Residuals	$\hat{\rho}$
NOYK	266	n.a.
NOYL	277	.48
KOYK	185	.40
KOYL 1	178	.37
LOF	(a)	.17
DIF 1	182	.11
DIF 2	182	.14
KOYLDIF	163	.08
KOYL 2	153	.21
KOYL 2 Yless[b]	178	.42

[a] Cannot be directly compared to the others.

[b] Not a finalist, but included as an important example which is referred to later in the text.

The standard error of estimate, a measure which enters into the standard error of forecast, was already made one of the chief criteria of selection. However, the accuracy of the forecast depends not only upon the size of the standard error of estimate, but also upon the deviation, in the forecast period, of the independent variables from their respective means. Those least squares estimates which boast the lowest standard error of estimate are therefore not guaranteed automatically the greatest success in forecasting.

Some predictions and actual figures are set out below. Attention is also drawn to Figs. 9 and 10 which give, in graphic form, an impression of the concordance of (retrospectively) predicted and actual sales for the regressions DIF and KOYL 2 respectively, for the period 1908–60.

A very severe forecasting test is to predict sales in the year 1935. As mentioned in Chap. 3, court litigation had as one of its consequences a precipitous drop of advertising expenditures (by about 45 per cent) from $1,504,000 in 1934 to $807,000 in 1935. Regressions not based on the cumulative effects model might be expected to predict a comparatively heavy drop in sales, while those embodying lagged effects (which place emphasis on advertising expenditure in the past as well as in the present) would be expected to forecast a lesser drop in sales. Table 13 offers comparisons of the predictive performances of the two groups of model versions with regard to 1935 sales. It seems fairly clear that the

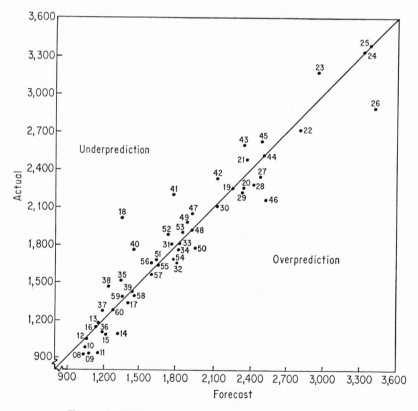

Fig. 9. DIF 2 forecast values *vs.* actual values (1908–1960)

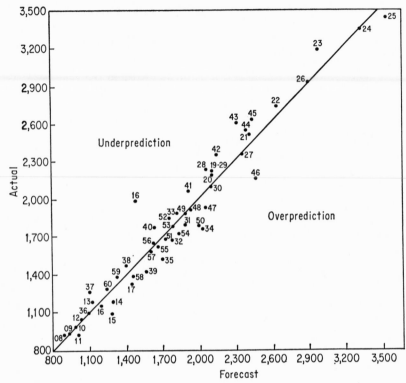

Fig. 10. Koyl 2 forecast values *vs.* actual values (1908–1960)

cumulative models give better predictions. If a summary performance measure of each of the two groups were required, the "measure of percentage error of forecast," to be referred to as MPE, could be pressed into service.[1] While developed to evaluate the predictive performance of a single regression, it can also serve for the purpose at hand:[2]

$$\text{MPE} = \sum \left| \frac{\text{actual} - \text{forecast}}{\text{actual}} \right| \Big/ \text{number of forecasts}$$

$$\text{MPE}_{1935} \text{ for non-cumulative models } = .157$$

$$\text{MPE}_{1935} \text{ for cumulative models } = .074$$

$$(\text{MPE}_{1935} \text{ for first difference models only } = .088)$$

---

[1] Ferber and Verdoorn, *op. cit.*, p. 476.

[2] Another possible measure of predictive performance is Theil's U, or inequality coefficient. See Theil, *op. cit.*, p. 32.

TABLE 13. FORECAST VS. ACTUAL SALES IN 1935[a]

(in $000)

(Actual Sales were 1,518)

Non-Cumulative Models			Cumulative Models		
Code Name	Forecast	Difference	Code Name	Forecast	Difference
DIF 2.B	1609	91	KOYL 2.B	1606	88
LOF .B	1662	144	KOYK .B	1416	-102
DIF 1.B	1351	-167	KOYL 2Y less .B	1647	129
NOYL .B	1135	-383	KOYL 1.B	1387	-131
NOYK .B	1112	-406			

LOF.B $\quad \Delta \log S_t = 3 + 220 \, \Delta \log A_t + 199 \, \Delta \log A_{t-1}$

NOYL .B $\quad S_t = -10{,}798 + 4105 \log A_t + 613D1 + 824D2$

NOYK .B $\quad S_t = -199 + 1.625A_t + 335D1 + 757D2$

KOYK .B $\quad S_t = -245 + .695S_{t-1} + .534A_t + 291D1 + 506D2$

KOYL 1.B $\quad S_t = -4479 + .638S_{t-1} + 1629 \log A_t + 434D1 + 562D2$

[a] 1908–34 (B) regression estimates not given in the text are set out below to permit calculation of forecasts. Both dummies have zero value in 1935.

The forecast of 1961 sales is of more practical interest than the 1935 prediction. Pinkham's spent $695,000 on advertising and realized sales of $1,426,000 in 1961. These figures became available in June, 1962 when, with unimportant exceptions, all regression calculations were completed.

Predictions of the various models are presented for comparison in Table 14. As can be seen from inspection and from the measure of percentage error, the cumulative effects models maintain their superiority over the other models.

$$\text{MPE}_{1961} \text{ for non-cumulative models} = .076$$

$$\text{MPE}_{1961} \text{ for cumulative models} = .042$$

$$(\text{MPE}_{1961} \text{ for first difference models only} = .043)$$

TABLE 14. 1908–60 REGRESSION FORECASTS VS. ACTUAL SALES IN 1961
(in $000)

Non-Cumulative Models			Cumulative Models		
		(Actual Sales Were 1,426)			
Code Name	Forecast	Difference	Code Name	Forecast	Difference
DIF 2	1465	39	KOYLDIF	1402	−24
LOF	1365	−61	KOYL 2 Yless	1453	27
DIF 1	1343	−83	KOYK	1395	−31
NOYL	1587	161	KOYL 1	1376	−50
NOYK	1620	194	KOYL 2	1257	−169

Attention is drawn to the excellent forecast by KOYL 2 Yless, the semi-logarithmic version of the cumulative effects model *without* disposable income. By comparison, KOYL 2, the version *with* disposable income, does less well. This instance illustrates the possibility of conflict between goodness of fit and predictive achievement. As was noted previously, the inclusion of disposable income, Y, into the cumulative semi-logarithmic model improved greatly the quality of the two attributes that were taken most seriously—it lowered the standard error of estimate and almost wholly removed autocorrelation among residuals. It is very likely, however, that much of the weak forecasting performance of KOYL 2 can be ascribed to the inclusion of Y, because disposable income in the forecast period was $365 billion, a considerable deviation from its mean value during the 1908–60 period, which was $110 billion.

TABLE 15. 1926–1960 REGRESSION FORECASTS VS. ACTUAL SALES IN 1961[a]

(in $000)

| | Non-Cumulative Models | | Cumulative Models | | |
| | (Actual Sales were 1,426) | | | | |
Code Name	Forecast	Difference	Code Name	Forecast[b]	Difference
LOF .C	1371	−55	KOYL 2 Yless .C	1426	0
DIF 1.C	1352	−74	KOYL 1.C	1448	22
NOYL .C	1655	229	KOYK .C	1453	27
NOYK .C	1677	251	KOYL 2.C	1274	−152

LOF .C $\quad \Delta \log S_t = 372\, \Delta \log A_t + 120\, \Delta \log A_{t-1}$

NOYL.C $\quad S_t = -5271 + 2437 \log A_t - 236D$

NOYK .C $\quad S_t = 886 + 1.138\, A_t - 331D$

KOYL 1.C $\quad S_t = -2680 + .520 S_{t-1} + 1217 \log A_t - 160D$

KOYK 1.C $\quad S_t = 376 + .529 S_{t-1} + .569 A_t - 197D$

[a] 1926–60 (C) regression estimates not given in the text are set out below to permit calculation of forecasts. The dummy has 0 value in 1961.

[b] The trend variable T assumed values 20 to 53 over the years covered.

It should nevertheless be stressed that this difference between fit and forecast occurs *within* the class of cumulative effects models and not *between* cumulative effects models and those which do not take delayed effects into consideration.

The forecasts of 1961 by the 1926–60 regressions are given in Table 15. DIF 2 and KOYLDIF models were not estimated for the 1926–60 period because of restricted time on the computer. Once again, the cumulative models predict better than the others:

MPE $(1926-60)_{1961}$ for non-cumulative models $= .107$

MPE $(1926-60)_{1961}$ for cumulative models $= .035$

MPE $(1926-60)_{1961}$ for first difference models only $= .045$

The 1926–60 series is probably to be preferred, as giving more accurate predictions, to the 1908–60 series. It encompasses a shorter period and is thus less exposed to changes that may have occurred in the characteristics of the underlying universe from which the sample observations are taken. Yet, with thirty-five observations it is comfortably long for statistical appraisal.

Table 16 represents an attempt to summarize the *predictive* performance of the regressions chosen for final consideration. However, it is only an incomplete substitute for the information given in the preceding pages and tables. By and large, it seems that the cumulative models give good account of themselves and tend to outperform the other models as regards forecasting.

A brief recapitulation of the *statistical* evidence on the alternative models is in order. When trying to explain the data, a regression that gives the best *fit* to them is to be looked for. By the various criteria that were employed (standard deviation of regression residuals, autocorrelation among residuals, magnitude of standard errors of regression coefficients, stability of results over time, etc.), the best fit to the Pinkham data was given by the regression family KOYL 2. This second-generation KOYL model version with one dummy, trend and disposable income embodies the cumulative effects model. It was chosen from among several hundred regression estimates and represents thus the outcome of exhaustive elimination.

As had been pointed out, the best explanation of past data is no automatic guarantee for best *prediction*, although the two are closely connected by the fact that good understanding of the past usually leads

TABLE 16. SUMMARY OF PREDICTIVE PERFORMANCE

Rank by Size of Difference between Actual and Forecast Sales

Code Name	1908–35	1908–61	1926–61
Non-Cumulative			
DIF 1	7	7	5
DIF 2	2	4	n.a.
LOF	6	6	4
NOYL	8	8	7
NOYK	9	10	8
Cumulative			
KOYL 2 Yless	4	2	1
KOYL 1	5	5	2
KOYL 2	1	9	6
KOYK	3	3	3
KOYLDIF	n.a.	1	n.a.
MPE non-cumulative	.157	.076	.107
MPE cumulative	.074	.042	.035
(MPE first difference only	.088	.043	.042)

to a good guess at the future.[1] Nevertheless, even in forecasting ability, the cumulative models tend to outperform the non-cumulative ones.

Some of the *economic* evidence on the cumulative models was already mentioned previously. Many regressions were eliminated because regression coefficients had "wrong" signs from the point of view of economic theory. Thus the process of narrowing down the choice was helped by a priori economic considerations. In periods dominated by high advertising expenditures (such as 1908–34), regression coefficients of the advertising variable were smaller than in periods not so dominated (such as 1908–60). This accords with theory, as it tends to show the operation of decreasing returns to a variable factor of the "production function." On this point it should also be noted that the semi-logarithmic functional forms of the regression models gave consistently better results than those in which the advertising variable was not used in logarithmic form.

---

[1] A thorough recent investigation into this matter is Mark B. Schupack, "The Predictive Accuracy of Empirical Demand Functions," *Economic Journal*, **LXXIII** (September, 1962), 550–75.

The 1935–36 episode, when advertising expenditures declined drastically as a result of the curtailment of Pinkham's managerial discretion, is interesting on two accounts. First, it shows that advertising did indeed have a major influence to play in stimulating sales—by no means a trivial point in advertising research—for sales declined considerably.[1]

Second, it tends to demonstrate, under extreme conditions, the soundness of the assumption of lagged effects, as the momentum of past advertising helped to sustain sales. The typical "naive" forecasting models (with which it is customary to confront tested models) are, in this case, NOYK and NOYL. The average of their forecasts under-predicts 1935 sales by $395,000, or 26 per cent, while the simple cumulative models KOYK and KOYL 1 give as an average of their forecasts $122,000 below actual sales, a difference of 8 per cent.

Are there other means of verifying the reasonableness, if not superiority, of the least squares estimates of the cumulative effects models? Wold points out that ". . . in regression analysis of non-experimental data the formal tests of significance, however refined, carry little weight as compared with the non-formal and non-quantitative significance that is embodied in results derived from independent sources, provided these results support one another and form an organic whole."[2] One parcel of supporting evidence coming from "independent" sources is based upon a survey which the company undertook in 1951. Questionnaires were inserted into liquid tonic packages asking, among other things, how long ago the buyer started using the compound. As a reward for answering a kitchen knife was offered. Two-thirds of those replying stated that they were using Pinkham's Compound for at least ten years (see Table 17). This is obviously too high a figure, since it is reasonable to expect that the response rate among old-time users may be much heavier than among new users. Also, there is likely to be the usually

---

[1] "Although statistical correlations, especially correlations involving lags, may give some evidence on direction of influence, they cannot be decisive . . . . In addition to statistical studies, . . . other kinds of studies are needed to judge with any confidence the direction of influence. Historical studies of particular episodes are especially valuable in this connection. The reason is that, in many episodes, attendant circumstances give strong evidence that changes in one or more of the variables were independent in origin." M. Friedman and J. Meiselman, "The Relative Stability of Monetary Velocity and the Investment Multiplier in the United States," (unpublished paper of the Workshop on Money and Banking of the University of Chicago, c. 1961).

[2] Wold, *op. cit.*, p. 58.

presumed bias imparted to such surveys by the tendency to please the questioner. Nevertheless, the results indicate a remarkable faithfulness to the compound. Whether this faithfulness is due to product quality and/or advertising (other things being equal) it is impossible to say. It certainly does not contradict the presumption that Pinkham's advertising does have a lagged effect upon sales.

TABLE 17. LENGTH OF USAGE OF THE VEGETABLE COMPOUND (RESULTS OF 1951 SURVEY OF RETURNED PACKAGE INSERTS)

		Started Using			
Survey Date	Number of Returned Inserts	During Past Year Percentage	Between 1941–50 Percentage	Before 1941 Percentage	No Answer Percentage
January	1765	27.7	30.4	39.2	2.7
March	1846	30.1	26.3	40.8	2.8
April	1311	30.7	24.1	41.8	3.4
Total	4922	29.5	27.2	40.5	2.8

Source: Company records.

Some economic implications of the results that are not immediately evident should also be explored. Dorfman and Steiner have shown the validity of the following rule for profit maximization. A firm should set the advertising appropriation and price for its product in such a way that the increase in gross revenue which will result from a one dollar increase in advertising should equal the price elasticity of the demand for the product:[1]

$$\frac{dS_t}{dA_t} = \text{price elasticity}$$

The first derivative of sales with respect to advertising was designated in Chap. 2 as the short-term marginal sales effect of advertising. It will be recalled that the long-term marginal sales effect of advertising was defined as the short-term effect divided by $1 - \lambda$. Table 18 shows the short- and long-term sales effects of the cumulative models. It can be seen that the company starts operating on the elastic portion of the demand curve only when the long-run sales effect is allowed to take

---

[1] R. Dorfman and P. O. Steiner, "Optimal Advertising and Optimal Quality," *American Economic Review*, **XLIV** (1954), 826–36.

place. Looking at only the short-term sales effect of advertising would
not give a rational explanation of the company's advertising policy.
Incidentally, the relatively low price elasticities which correspond to
the sales effects provide circumstantial evidence of Pinkham's monopoly
position.

TABLE 18. SHORT- AND LONG-TERM MARGINAL SALES EFFECTS OF 1908–60 CUMULATIVE
EFFECT REGRESSIONS

(based on av A_t = \$941,000)

	Short-term	Long-term
KOYK	.537	1.44
KOYL 1	.566[a]	1.54[b]
KOYL 2	.545	1.63
KOYL 2 Yless	.610	1.80

[a] $(dS_t/d \log_{10} \text{av } A_t)$ = .4343 $\hat{\alpha}$/av A_t = (.4343)(1226)/(941).
[b] $(dS_e/d \log_{10} \text{av } A_t)$ = .4343 $\hat{\alpha}$/(av A_t)(1 − $\hat{\lambda}$) = (.4343) (1226)/(941)(.367).

The relation of the long-term marginal sales effect to price elasticity,
given profit-maximizing behavior, leads to a consideration of the size
of annual advertising outlays. The starting point is the condition that a
monopolist will not operate on the inelastic portion of the demand curve
facing him. The lowest price elasticity—and thus long-term marginal
sales effect—above which he can conceivably break even is 1. The
formula which gives the long-term marginal sales effect of advertising
is, in the case of the semi-logarithmic equations

$$\text{MSE}_{\text{LT}} = \frac{\alpha(.4343)/A_i}{1 - \lambda}$$

Setting this expression equal to 1, the "break-even" value of A_i is
$(.4343)/1 - \lambda$. In the case of the 1908–60 KOYL 2 estimates this value
is about \$1,530,000. It is interesting to note that the company, in the
context of these particular regression estimates, "overspent" on advertising only five times during the 53 years: in 1924, 1925, 1926, 1929
and 1930. Thus the line of reasoning, leading from the implications of
profit-maximizing behavior in advertising situations to certain numerical
outcomes, tends to support indirectly the results given by the cumulative
model regressions.

The notion of "break-even" advertising elasticity can also be ex-
ploited to some purpose. As far as can be determined, Pinkham's total
expenses exclusive of advertising and capital costs averaged 25 per cent

TABLE 19. ADVERTISING ELASTICITIES OF SELECTED 1908–60 REGRESSIONS AND THEIR
PROFIT IMPLICATIONS

Code Name	Advertising Elasticity at Sample Means	Change in Profits[a]
NOYK	.723	$ 578
NOYL	.741[b]	815
DIF 1	.530	−2,500
DIF 2	.560	−2,440
LOF	.499[c]	−1,675

	Short-Run	Long-Run	
KOYK	.274	.736	760[d]
KOYL 1	.289	.788[e]	1,375[d]
KOYL 2	.279	.831	2,060[d]
KOYL 2 Yless	.310	.915	4,136[d]

[a] Increase in pre-tax profit that can be obtained by increasing advertising expenditure by 1 per cent over the average sample figure. For the NOYK–NOYL series mean sales are $1,835,000 and mean advertising expenditures $935,000. For all others they are $1,840,000 and $941,000, respectively.

[b] $(dS_t/d \log_{10} \text{av } A_t)$ $(\text{av } A_t/\text{av } S_t) = (.4343\hat{\alpha}/\text{av } A_t)$

$(\text{av } A_t/\text{av } S_t) = .4343\hat{\alpha}/\text{av } S_t = (.4343) (3120)/1835.$

[c] Actually a "longer-run" elasticity calculated by simply adding the coefficients of the two advertising variables: .328 and .171.

[d] Computed from long-run elasticities.

[e] $(dS_e/d \log_{10} \text{av } A_t)$ $(\text{av } A_t/\text{av } S_t) = \dfrac{.4343\hat{\alpha}/\text{av } A_t}{1 - \hat{\lambda}} \dfrac{\text{av } A_t}{\text{av } S_t}$

$$= .4343\hat{\alpha}/(1 - \hat{\lambda}) (\text{av } S_t) = (.4343) (1226)/(.367) (1840) \cdot$$

of sales over the whole period covered. At the sample mean values of advertising ($941,000) and sales ($1,840,000), it can be calculated that the lowest advertising elasticity of demand which would give the company a profit must exceed .68, since, for a 1 per cent increase in advertising at this level, the following relationship must be satisfied:

(elasticity) (sales revenue)

$$> \text{(elasticity) (sales revenue) } (.25) + \text{ ad costs}$$

$$(E) (\$18,400) > (E) \ \$18,400) (.25) + \$9,410$$

From Table 19 it is obvious that only by taking the "long view" does advertising become a paying proposition at Pinkham's. The first-difference results are difficult to interpret in this context, except that intuitively it could be expected that they would lie somewhere between the short-run and long-run values, and that they do. The column "Change in Profits" was inserted into the table in order to permit a "dollar-and-cents" comparison of the various advertising elasticities.

The last question to be asked is whether the estimates obtained with the help of the cumulative models look reasonable in view of its investment implications. The marginal rate of return on the invested advertising dollar was defined in Chap. 2 as

$$r = \frac{c\alpha + \lambda - 1}{1 - c}$$

where c is 1 *minus* all costs, except advertising, as per cent of sales.[1] (All expenses, except advertising and capital costs, are estimated to average 25 per cent of sales over the whole period, giving a c equal to .75.) This rate represents the contribution of advertising expenditure *at the margin* to the *pre-tax* rate of return on the company's capital. Estimated rates of return on the advertising dollar invested at the margin for the year 1961 are set out in Table 20.

TABLE 20. ESTIMATES OF 1961 MARGINAL ADVERTISING RATES OF RETURN[a]

	Based on 1908–60 Regression Estimates	Based on 1926–60 Regression Estimates
KOYK	.052	− .077
KOYL 1	.470[b]	.256
KOYL 2	.484	.500
KOYL 2 Yless	.553	.238

[a] 1961 advertising outlay was $695,000.

$$\text{[b]} \left[\frac{(.75)(1226)(.4343)}{695} + .633 - 1 \right] \div \left[1 - \frac{(.75)(1226)(.4343)}{695} \right].$$

The KOYK estimates are derived from a linear function, thus expressing an average for the whole period. They cannot, therefore, be directly compared to the other estimates. Estimates derived from the semi-logarithmic functions appear consistent and plausible. A return on investment of about 25 per cent *after tax* seems about par for the proprietary drug industry.

---

[1] When the regression is of semi-logarithmic form, the short-run marginal sales effect, $.4343\alpha/A_i$, should be substituted for α.

An *average* of marginal rates was calculated from the KOYL 2 estimates. For the period 1908–34, dominated by high advertising expenditures, it is .156. The average of the 1926–60 estimates of marginal rates (a period in which very high advertising outlays were less predominant than in 1908–34) is .330. The mean for the period 1908–60 is .530, the highest of the three periods. This again conforms to expectations, because very large annual advertising outlays were not as frequent as during the other two periods. During this longest period taxes took, as a rough estimate, about 30 per cent of the company's profits. This would leave a net rate of return of approximately 37 per cent—again, not an implausible figure for a well-established monopolist.[1]

"Since every econometric analysis is an essay in persuasion—just as is true for any other branch of science—the line of thought leading to the finally accepted result must be expounded."[2] The line of thought pursued in the foregoing pages led to the affirmation of the potential usefulness of the cumulative effects approach in the measurement of advertising effectiveness. It is hoped that it was expounded skillfully enough to persuade the reader.

---

[1] The rate of return on the company's total capital will be lower than that, if the firm's whole investment base is considered and if advertising brings in the highest return of all resource factors. Not much more, though, because in Pinkham's case investment in plant and other assets is relatively small compared to its advertising "assets."

[2] Theil, *op. cit.*, p. 207.

CHAPTER 6

Summary and Conclusions

The major objective of this study was to determine whether the measurement of cumulative advertising effects could be attempted or improved by having recourse to the model of distributed lags proposed by Koyck. A corollary objective was to ascertain, in a particular instance, the existence, importance, and measurability of long-run effects of advertising. To this end an econometric investigation was undertaken of the marketing operations of Lydia E. Pinkham Medicine Company over a period of fifty-odd years.

In the introductory chapter the proposition is entertained that not enough research is being undertaken into the effects of the firm's advertising outlays upon its sales. Evidence, gathered from a survey of many professional journals, is adduced in support of this claim. The great difficulty of isolating the net influence of advertising expenditure on revenue frequently leads advertisers to rest content with "limited objective" research. In such research, a single ingredient of the advertising effort is selected for scrutiny and evaluated in terms of an effect deemed not too "distant" from it. "Limited objective" research is based on two propositions: (1) the productivity of each advertising input (e.g., copy, media vehicle) can be evaluated separately from the productivity of the other advertising inputs, and, (2) there is a unidirectional, hierarchical sequence of effects (e.g., recall, favorable attitude, etc.) that leads from exposure to advertisements on to purchase.

Mass communications theory fails to support either proposition. Economic production theory would reject the first one, if complementarity or substitutability were postulated for the various advertising input factors. More importantly, however, "limited objective" research cannot go beyond the estimation of the individual marginal revenue products of advertising inputs. While this may be useful in arriving at the least-cost combination of the resources that go into the advertising production function, it cannot provide an answer to the question of how much a firm should spend on advertising. If the firm is to maximize the present value of its net receipts, it must allocate its budget among competing ends such as plant, inventories, research and advertising in such a way as to equate the marginal rate of return on capital with the marginal cost of it. This definitely requires the estimation (albeit often of an informal nature) of the shape of the total advertising production function, frequently in a multi-period context. Such an estimation can only be based upon "total effect" research into the influence of advertising expenditure on sales.

If the existence of long-run effects is suspected, time-series analysis may be the method of "total effect" advertising research which is preferable to short-period experimental studies and cross-sectional analyses. However, the "traditional" way of regressing sales on advertising expenditure does not necessarily take into account the existence of carry-over advertising effects. Students of advertising, giving psychological and institutional reasons, have maintained for years that many kinds of advertising have cumulative effects. Lagged or cumulative effects of advertising may be defined as: (1) the effects of a perceived advertisement which influences two or more successive purchasing decisions of a consumer with regard to a given product (or brand of a product), or (2) the effects of an advertisement which influences consumer buying behavior beyond the period of its appearance.

Theoretical articles concerned with this phenomenon are not lacking, but empirical investigations are scant. If lagged effects are present in many advertising situations, it follows that an important gap exists in advertising research.

As is explained in the second chapter, complicated and unsatisfactory methods hampered the measurement of distributed lags (as lagged or cumulative effects are often called) until the Dutch econometrician Koyck published his monograph *Distributed Lags and Investment Analysis* in 1954. He proposed the working hypothesis that the reaction of the dependent variable assumes the distribution of a geometric progression from a certain time period onward. The simplest case is one in which the effect of the independent upon the dependent variable starts declining in a constant proportion from the first period on.

As an example, the sales revenue of a firm may depend linearly on both current and past advertising outlays:

$$S_t = a + \beta_1 A_t + \beta_2 A_{t-1} + \beta_3 A_{t-2} + \cdots + u_t$$

where $\beta_1 = \alpha$; $\beta_2 = \alpha\lambda$; $\beta_3 = \alpha\lambda^2$; $0 < \lambda < 1$; and S stands for sales revenue, A for advertising expenditures and u for disturbance, all in periods designated by the subscripts.

Before the advent of Koyck's distributed lag model the investigator did not usually place restrictions on the beta coefficients, of which he estimated as many as he judged necessary. Koyck's approach simplifies matters considerably. Re-write (1), then lag it one period and multiply it by λ to obtain (2). Subtract (2) from (1) to get (3).

(1) $$S_t = a + \alpha A_t + \alpha\lambda A_{t-1} + \alpha\lambda^2 A_{t-2} + \cdots + u_t$$

(2) $$\lambda S_{t-1} = \lambda a + \alpha\lambda A_{t-1} + \alpha\lambda^2 A_{t-2} + \cdots + \lambda u_{t-1}$$

(3) $$S_t = (1 - \lambda)a + \alpha A_t + \lambda S_{t-1} + u_t - \lambda u_{t-1}$$

Several advantages are claimed for this model. Typically, the "traditional" models that embody the concept of distributed lags use a considerable number of (lagged) exogenous variables, while the simple Koyck model uses only one lagged and one non-lagged exogenous variable. If this substantially simpler model were to give nearly as good a picture of reality, it may be preferable to employ it. For instance, the fact that Koyck's model does not use a variable in several lagged versions (e.g., A_t, A_{t-1}, A_{t-2}, etc.) means that it is less exposed to such potential consequences of multicollinearity as increase in measurement error and lowered reliability of individual parameter estimates. Use of the model is also apt to reduce the autocorrelation among residuals which is so often present in regression analysis of economic time-series.[1] The idea that advertising effects decline exponentially (frequently encountered in theoretical advertising literature) allows the development of the concept of advertising capital. Sometimes also called stock of consumer goodwill, it is built-up over several periods and depreciates at the rate of $1 - \lambda$. The notion of exponentially declining effects, encouraging the investment perspective of advertising, leads also to the definition of the marginal rate of return on the dollar invested in advertising, $c\alpha + \lambda - 1/1 - c\alpha$, where c is *1 minus* all costs except ad-

---

[1] If $v_t = u_t - \kappa u_{t-1} + \epsilon_t$ and κ approaches λ, v_t approaches ϵ_t. The latter is defined, in this first-order autoregressive scheme, as a serially independent random variable with a finite, constant variance.

vertising, as per cent of sales. A neat distinction can also be made between short-run (α) and long-run ($\alpha/1 - \lambda$) marginal sales effects of advertising which, in turn, lead to the calculation of the respective advertising elasticities of sales.

The fundamental question is, however, whether Koyck's model of distributed lags expresses better than any heretofore employed implicit models the mechanism by which advertising influences sales over time. It was the task of this dissertation to answer this question by examining the statistical *fit* of this model (and other "traditional" models) to a set of actual data and by looking at its *predictive* ability. With that in view, an empirical study was made of the economic environment and relevant commercial operations of Lydia E. Pinkham Medicine Company between the years 1908 and 1960.

Pinkham was chosen for intensive investigation for several reasons. The firm spent a very high proportion (40–60 per cent) of its sales on advertising. Furthermore, it did not employ many of the customary "parameters" of marketing action: sales force, credit, discounts, frequent changes in package, point of purchase efforts, special offerings, etc. The assumption thus could safely be made that advertising had a measurable effect on Pinkham's sales. The product itself, Lydia Pinkham's Vegetable Compound, had no close substitutes. Competitors' marketing action was not, therefore, a complicating factor to be coped with. By the same token certain allied issues, such as the geographic distribution of Pinkham's marketing effort could be ignored. During the detailed examination which followed the decision to delve into the Pinkham case further factors were discovered which added to the simplicity of the ultimate quantitative analysis. On the whole the conclusion was reached that there was remarkable stability (between 1907–60) in the universe from which the sample observations were obtained.

Thanks to the generous and candid attitude of Pinkham's management it was possible to examine all the issues considered relevant. Most important of all, monthly sales and advertising figures covering the years 1907–1960 were obtained. This was one of the weightiest reasons leading to the study of Lydia Pinkham, as data on advertising expenditures of individual brands are extremely difficult to get.

The pertinent history of the Lydia Pinkham Medicine Company, with particular reference to changes in marketing policies, is outlined in the third chapter, while the fourth chapter has the task of preparing the ground for multiple regression analysis of sales and advertising.

Current dollars were chosen as the units in which to measure sales and advertising, because the changing product mix of the vegetable compound (sold in liquid and tablet form) precluded measurement in physical units and no satisfactory deflators of advertising outlay and sales revenue could be found.

A year was settled upon as the proper time unit for regression analysis in preference to a month. Some other exogenous variables which are to be controlled for (e.g., disposable income) are not available in monthly form over the entire fifty-three year period. Errors of observation are more likely to occur with the use of monthly data. There are no a priori, extra-statistical grounds to favor the shorter period. Finally, regression analysis of monthly data during a sample period (1954–60) did not support the use of monthly data.

The larger part of the fourth chapter deals with the screening out of certain variables. Consumption of spirits, price, nature of product changes, marketing channels, and the relative importance of media employed were among the factors considered and rejected as candidate exogenous variables for the multiple regression analysis of Pinkham's sales. Price, customarily deemed the most important element in the demand function, did not qualify on two grounds: changes in the factory price were not systematically reflected at retail (the Compound being a favorite loss leader), yet prices at retail could not be ascertained; and prices at factory changed so seldom that their inclusion in a multi-variate analysis was at best questionable. There remained (aside from advertising outlays) disposable income, dummies representing quality of the advertising copy and, occasionally, trend as exogenous variables to be used in the regression analysis.

The fifth chapter presents and evaluates results of the regression analysis. Koyck's model of distributed lags is set up in several versions and its parameters are estimated by least squares from the Pinkham data. Its ability to explain, as well as to predict, movements in the company's sales is judged by various statistical criteria. Implications of the results are assessed in the light of economic theory. In addition, the model is also appraised by comparing it to alternative models which are applied to the same set of data.

The simplest version of the cumulative effects model is

$$S_t = a + \alpha A_t + \lambda S_{t-1} \qquad \text{(KOYK)}$$

A slight difference is introduced if the advertising variable is used in logarithmic form to express a belief that there are decreasing returns to advertising:

$$S_t = a + \alpha \log A_t + \lambda S_{t-1} \qquad \text{(KOYL)}$$

The first alternative model, in its simple and semi-logarithmic form, can perhaps be called the traditional model for the regression measurement of advertising effectiveness:

$$S_t = a + \alpha A_t \quad \text{(NOYK)}, \qquad S_t = a + \alpha \log A_t \quad \text{(NOYL)}$$

The second alternative model employs first differences instead of the original data. It has proved successful in many analyses of economic time-series, where its use tends to reduce the serial correlation so often found in the data:

$$\Delta S_t = a + \Delta A_t \quad \text{(DIF)}, \qquad \Delta \log S_t = a + \Delta \log A_t \quad \text{(LOF)}$$

The third model is a logarithmic form of the first difference model. However, due to a computer programming error, the dependent variable was also converted into logarithms and as a consequence the performance of this model cannot be easily compared to that of the others.

Up to five more exogenous variables are used in the regression analysis of the models: three dummies which represent (by assuming the values of 1 and 0) four different eras of advertising copy at Pinkham's, time trend and disposable income. To check the consistency of the results, regressions were run on all model versions for the subperiods 1908–40, 1908–34 and 1926–60, in addition to the basic period of analysis which spanned the years 1908–60.

The very large number of regression estimates necessitates the adoption of a step-by-step elimination of uninteresting results. In the end, one or several "best" regressions of each basic model are chosen and entered into "finals" for comparison and evaluation.

First, the possibility has to be considered that the postulated reaction in the cumulative effects model does not get underway immediately, but only after one or two periods. This requires the inclusion of at least two past years of advertising expenditure. To give the other models the same chance, NOYK's and NOYL's are also estimated with A_{t-1} and A_{t-2}, while the first difference models (DIF's and LOF's) are estimated with up to A_{t-4}. (All estimation takes place within the basic period as well as the sub-periods.)

A simplified summary of the regressions run can be set out as

$$S_t = [S_{t-1}] + (\log)\ A_t + (\log)\ A_{t-1} + (\log)\ A_{t-2}$$
$$+ D1 + D2 + D3 + T$$

KOYK or (KOYL) or [NOYK] or [(NOYL)]

$$\Delta \log S_t = \Delta\ (\log)\ A_t + \Delta\ (\log A_{t-1}) + \cdots + \Delta\ (\log)\ A_{t-4}$$
$$+D1 + D2 + D3$$

DIF or (LOF)

T(rend) and D(ummies) are dropped successively, then the lagged advertising variable farthest to the right is omitted and T and Ds reinstated, and so on.

The inclusion of the lagged advertising variables either increases the standard deviation of the regression residuals (and so reduces the explanation of the variation in the dependent variable), or it results in negative signs of their regression coefficients. This pattern generally holds for all models and all periods, with the exception of the DIF and LOF models with A_{t-1}. Almost 150 regression estimates were thus calculated to arrive at the conclusion that the Koyck model *with* lagged advertising variables need not be considered further.

The remaining regression estimates are evaluated first on the magnitude of their standard deviation of regression residuals. The standard error of estimate not only gives a good measure of fit, but is also the only regression measure related to the predictive ability of the regression equation (as judged by the standard error of forecast). Once the "finalists" are chosen, they are also subjected to an evaluation of independence among regression residuals. This is achieved following the time-consuming computation of the Durbin–Watson statistic. Where signs of non-independence among successive residuals are detected, doubt is cast upon the proper specification of the model.

Regression estimates kept for final comparison and analysis are set out below:

NOYK:

$$S_t = 634 + 1.418A_t - 338D1 + 131D2 - 393D3$$

$$(.112) \qquad (124) \qquad (98) \qquad (94)$$
633 266

$$N = 54 \qquad R^2 = .836$$

NOYL:

$$S_t = -7280 + 3120 \log A_t - 220D1 + 225D2 - 281D3$$

$$\begin{matrix} & (260) & (134) & (101) & (96) \\ 633 & & & & 277 \end{matrix}$$

$$N = 54 \qquad R^2 = .823 \qquad d = 1.04 \qquad \hat{\rho} = .48$$

DIF 1:

$$\Delta S_t = -16 + .531\Delta A_t + 51D1 + 156D2 - 62D3$$

$$\begin{matrix} & (124) & (.119) & (84) & (95) & (79) \\ 236 & & & & & 182 \end{matrix}$$

$$N = 53 \qquad R^2 = .456 \qquad d = 1.78 \qquad \hat{\rho} = .11$$

DIF 2:

$$\Delta S_t = -102 + .562\Delta A_t - 144D$$

$$\begin{matrix} & (.117) & (54) \\ 236 & & 182 \end{matrix}$$

$$N = 53 \qquad R^2 = .405 \qquad d = 1.71 \qquad \hat{\rho} = .14$$

LOF:

$$\Delta \log S_t = -5 + 328\Delta \log A_t + 171\Delta \log A_{t-1}$$

$$\begin{matrix} & (86) & (60) & (60) \\ 58.0 & & & 44.6 \end{matrix}$$

$$N = 52 \qquad R^2 = .431 \qquad d = 1.65 \qquad \hat{\rho} = .17$$

KOYK:

$$S_t = 212 + .628S_{t-1} + .537A_t - 102D1 + 181D2 - 203D3$$

$$\begin{matrix} & (.085) & (.143) & (98) & (68) & (70) \\ 629 & & & & & 185 \end{matrix}$$

$$N = 53 \qquad R^2 = .922 \qquad d = 1.19 \qquad \hat{\rho} = .41$$

KOYL 1:

$$S_t = -2924 + .633S_{t-1} + 1226 \log A_t - 20D1 + 215D2 - 164D3$$

$$\begin{matrix} & (.075) & (282) & (93) & (65) & (63) \\ 629 & & & & & 178 \end{matrix}$$

$$N = 53 \qquad R^2 = .928 \qquad d = 1.27 \qquad \hat{\rho} = .37$$

KOYLDIF:

$$S_t - .37 S_{t-1} = -1903 + .527 (S_{t-1} - .37 S_{t-2})$$
$$(.085)$$
415

$$+ 1326 (\log A_t - .37 \log A_{t-1}) - 41D1 + 165D2 + 108D3$$

(276)   (84)   (60)   (57)
163

$$N = 53 \qquad R^2 = .864 \qquad d = 1.83 \qquad \hat{\rho} = .08$$

KOYL 2:

$$S_t = -3649 + .665 S_{t-1} + 1180 \log A_t + 774D + 32T - 2.83Y$$

(.063)   (243)   (107)   (5.9)   (.67)
629   153

$$N = 53 \qquad R^2 = .941 \qquad d = 1.59 \qquad \hat{\rho} = .20$$

KOYL 2:
Yless:

$$S_t = -3663 + .661 S_{t-1} + 1314 \log A_t + 482D + 9.8T$$

(.073)   (280)   (95)   (2.9)
629   178

$$N = 53 \qquad R^2 = .920 \qquad d = 1.16 \qquad \hat{\rho} = .42$$

(Ds stand for dummies, T for trend, Y for disposable income, N for sample size, R^2 for unadjusted coefficient of determination, d for the Durbin–Watson statistic, $\hat{\rho}$ for the estimated coefficient of autocorrelation. Figures in parentheses are standard errors of regression coefficients. Figures on the line immediately below them are the standard deviations of the dependent variable and of the regression residuals.)

Regressions designated by 2 (e.g., DIF 2) were estimated in a second round of computer calculations, when it became apparent that only one dummy would suffice to explain the variations in copy quality. Disposable consumer income is also included in the second generation estimates, but fails to improve the quality of the DIF 2 estimates. It is not retained in the KOYL 2 Yless estimates.

The first five regressions represent the best-fitting estimates of each of the non-cumulative models, mainly as judged by the size of their standard errors of regression residuals. Among the last five, KOYK, KOYL 1 and KOYL 2 are the best-fitting versions of the cumulative effects models. KOYLDIF is a modified first-difference transformation of KOYL 1, based on the estimated auto-correlation coefficient of that regression. KOYL 2 Yless is included because of its anticipated excellent forecasting performance.

Of all the regressions computed in the course of this investigation, the KOYL 2 series has by far the lowest standard deviations of residuals in each of the four periods (leading its nearest competitors by $10,000 to $25,000). The group of the five equations which represent the cumulative effects model also leads decisively in predictive ability. Forecasts are made for the year 1935, in which there was a drastic reduction of advertising expenditure from previous levels, and for the year 1961. (At the time of calculation results for that year were not known yet.) The briefest of summaries of the predictive results appears below:

	1908–35	Forecast off by	1908–61	Forecast off by	1926–61	Forecast off by
Best forecast	KOYL 2	5.8%	KOYLDIF	1.7%	KOYL 2 Yless	0.0%
Second best	DIF 2	6.0%	KOYL 2 Yless	1.9%	KOYL 1	1.5%
Third best	KOYK	6.7%	KOYK	2.2%	KOYK	1.9%
MPE non-cumulative	15.7%		7.6%		10.7%	
MPE cumulative	7.4%		4.2%		3.5%	
(MPE first difference only	8.8%		4.3%		4.5%)	

MPE, or measure of percentage error, was calculated for the two groups of model estimates by the formula

$$\sum \left| \frac{\text{actual} - \text{forecast}}{\text{actual}} \right| \bigg/ \text{number of forecasts}$$

Only DIF 2 appears once among the best three forecasts for each "period," while the MPE's of the non-cumulative models are uniformly larger than those of their rivals.

The excellent forecasting performance of KOYL 2 Yless should be noted. The exclusion of disposable income brings in its wake a considerable increase in the coefficient of autocorrelation—from .20 for KOYL 2 to .42 for KOYL 2 Yless. The model estimates do not *fit* the data as well any more. However, there is now no longer a variable present in the model, whose value in the forecasting period is far removed from its mean value. As the mean value of disposable income in the period 1908–60 is $119 billion and in the forecasting period it is $365 billion, this may be the explanation of the good predictive performance of KOYL 2 Yless compared to that of KOYL 2. This instance provides an example of the potential conflict between the criteria of goodness of fit and predictive ability. However, it is worth stressing that *the distributed lag models both give a better fit to the Pinkham data and forecast better than the models which do not incorporate lagged effects.*

When looked at from the economic viewpoint, the cumulative models also give good account of themselves. When, in 1935, advertising expenditures were slashed, sales did not decline as much as the non-cumulative models predicted they would. This tends to demonstrate the soundness of the assumption of lagged effects, as the momentum of past advertising helps to sustain sales. A questionnaire survey undertaken by the company in 1951 revealed that the majority of Pinkham's customers has been using the vegetable compound for at least ten years. This apparent faithfulness does not contradict the assumption that the effects of a Pinkham advertisement influence two or more successive purchasing decisions of some of its customers.

The Dorfman-Steiner theorem relates the optimal size of advertising expenditure to the price-elasticity of demand. Estimates of the marginal sales effect of advertising show that only when the *long-term* effects $(\alpha/1 - \lambda)$ are allowed to work out does the company start operating on the price-elastic portion of its demand curve. The proposition that a monopolist will not operate on the inelastic portion of the demand curve leads to the consideration of the size of the maximum "rational" advertising outlays. It is shown that the company exceeded this limit only five times during the fifty-three years surveyed. The notion of "breakeven" advertising elasticity is introduced and leads to the conclusion that only in the long run did it pay to advertise at Pinkham's.

Algebraic signs of the partial regression coefficients do not violate a priori expectations. In periods dominated by high advertising expenditures (such as 1908–34), regression coefficients of the advertising variable are smaller than in periods not so dominated (such as 1908–60). This accords with theory, as it tends to confirm the operation of decreasing returns to a variable factor.

Perhaps the most convincing indirect support of the distributed lag model comes from estimates of the marginal rates of return on the invested advertising dollar. An average of marginal rates was calculated for the KOYL 2 series. For the period 1908–34, dominated by high advertising outlays, it is 15.6 per cent. For 1926–60 it is 33 per cent, and for 1908–60 it reaches 53 per cent. If it is estimated that taxes took roughly 30 per cent of the company's profits during the longest period, a post-tax rate of return of approximately 37 per cent is obtained. This is not an implausible figure for a well-established monopolist. The 1961 pre-tax rate of return given by the 1908–60 estimates is about 50 per cent, while that given by the 1926–60 estimates varies between 27 and 50 per cent, depending on the model version.

The major and the corollary objectives of this study appear to have been attained. It seems that the measurement of cumulative effects can be successfully attempted with the help of Koyck's model of distributed lags. Using the distributed lag approach, first the existence and then the relative importance of the operation of lagged advertising effects is all but confirmed in the case of a successful advertiser.

These findings are of importance to advertising research. The hypothesis that lagged effects exist—and may be important—finds another, by no means frequent, confirmation. Also, a potentially useful tool of analysis is added to the still quite meager equipment of investigators who try to measure the "total" effect of advertising on sales. There is nothing that would preclude the application of this tool in other advertising situations, where delayed effects are suspected to exist. In particular, there do not seem to be any product characteristics which would, *per se*, make the distributed lag model more or less applicable. It is clear that the analysis pursued here cannot be applied without some modification to other markets, but this is true of the great majority of measurement techniques in advertising. An illustration may be of help. It was noted that the monopoly position of Lydia Pinkham's made for a simpler approach than would have been necessary in an oligopolistic situation. Such a situation would have probably called for the use of market-share type of data, instead of absolute dollar figures.[1] Nevertheless, there would have been no reason to change the basic distributed lag model *because of the different market structure.*

Koyck's model of distributed lags has been applied in various areas of economics, such as demand and expectations analysis. It is shown that it has potentially useful application in managerial economics as well. Students of imperfect competition who believe that advertising expenditures sometimes create barriers to entry may, with the help of the approach propounded here, examine the quantitative and dynamic implications of their assertions.

---

[1] Telser, *loc. cit.*

Appendix

Table 21 shows estimates of per capita consumption of absolute alcohol (per capita figures are easier to obtain than absolute figures). The basic source of per capita consumption figures is the yearly *United States Statistical Abstracts*. These figures are given for distilled spirits, malt beverages (beer) and wines, in gallons. They were converted to gallons of absolute alcohol by using the Yale Alcohol Research Center method: distilled spirits are deemed to contain 45 per cent of pure alcohol on the average, wines 17 per cent and beer 4 per cent.[1] The *Abstracts* do not, however, list any alcohol consumption for the prohibition years, which is patently absurd. Estimates covering the years 1919 to 1930 had to be taken from Clark Warburton's doctoral dissertation at Columbia, which gives per capita gallons of pure alcohol, but uses a slightly different conversion system.[2] Warburton assigns a 50 per cent alcoholic content to distilled spirits, 10 per cent to wine and 4 per cent to beer. However, since his most reliable estimates appear in the pure alcohol version only, it is impossible to bring the *Abstracts'* and his estimates to an identical base.

Warburton estimated the consumption of alcohol during the Prohibition in three ways. He estimated a regression equation of per capita pure alcohol consumption on several raw materials used in the manufacture of alcoholic beverages during a dozen years preceding the dry era. These least squares estimates were then assumed to hold from 1920 to 1930 and production figures of the raw materials (hops, grapes, etc.) substituted into the equation. The results were corrected for published figures of seized caches of alcohol and Canadian statistics of alcoholic beverage exports to the United States. Similar procedure was adopted with respect to death rates from alcoholism and to arrests for drunkenness. Finally, Warburton combined the three different estimates

---

[1] E. M. Jellinek, "Recent Trends in Alcoholism and Alcohol Consumption," *Quarterly Journal of Studies on Alcohol*, **VIII** (1947–48), No. 1, 1–60.

[2] Clark Warburton, *The Economic Results of Prohibition* (New York: Columbia University Press, 1932).

TABLE 21. U.S. PER CAPITA CONSUMPTION OF ABSOLUTE ALCOHOL, 1908–1960
(in gallons)

Year	Gallons	Year	Gallons
1908	1.50[a]	1934	.64[e]
09	1.50	35	.85
1910	1.57	36	1.00
11	1.58	37	1.07
12	1.58	38	1.03
13	1.59	39	1.04
14	1.44	1940	1.08
15	1.39	41	1.15
16	1.46	42	1.25
17	1.30	43	1.29
18	.91	44	1.36
19	.77[b]	45	1.47
1920	.64[c]	46	1.48
21	.54	47	1.39
22	.91	48	1.34
23	1.07	49	1.32
24	1.05	1950	1.34
25	1.10	51	1.32
26	1.18	52	1.28
27	1.12	53	1.32
28	1.18	54	1.30
29	1.20	55	1.29
1930	1.06	56	1.30
31	.96[d]	57	1.28
32	.85	58	1.27
33	.74	59	1.29
		1960	1.29

[a] U.S. Department of Commerce, *Statistical Abstract of the United States, 1921* (Washington, D.C., 1922), p. 616. The *Abstracts* give gallonage figures for distilled spirits, malt beverages and wines. These figures were converted into gallons of pure alcohol by multiplying the gallons of distilled spirits by a factor of .45, malt beverages by .04 and wines by .17.

[b] Linear interpolation between the *Abstract's* and Warburton's estimates.

[c] Clark Warburton, *The Economic Results of Prohibition* (New York: Columbia University Press, 1932), Table 45.

[d] 1931–1933 estimates are linear interpolations between Warburton's and the *Abstracts'* estimates.

[e] From 1934 to 1958 the estimates are taken and converted from various *Abstracts*. The 1959 and 1960 estimates are averages of the years 1954–1958.

and it is these pooled estimates for the years 1920 to 1930 that are used here.[1]

The years 1919 and 1931, 1932 and 1933 are linear interpolations between the figures given in the *Abstracts* and by Warburton and as such thoroughly unsatisfactory. The year 1934, as given in the *Abstracts*, cannot be considered reliable either, because unofficial production still rivaled the output of the reopened distilleries and breweries. Finally, the figures for the years 1959 and 1960 were obtained by averaging the years 1954 to 1958.

There is thus a period of at least sixteen years (1919–1935) during which the accuracy of observations upon the contemplated exogenous variable is very much open to question. Since so much work was devoted to the sifting and assembly of the alcohol consumption data, it was only with great reluctance that it was decided not to consider this variable in the final regressions. The fact must be faced, however, that one-third of the observations is simply too unreliable. Nonetheless, as some computational work was already done, it might be mentioned that the simple correlation coefficients between total sales (i.e., liquid *and* tablets) and per capita alcohol consumption are minus .38 for the fifty-three years, minus .48 for the period 1908 to 1940, and minus .56 for 1908 to 1934. They can be considered significant by conventional standards.

---

[1] *Ibid.*, Table 45.

Selected Bibliography

Books

Borden, Neil H. *The Economic Effects of Advertising.* Homewood, Ill.: Richard D. Irwin, Inc., 1952.

——. *Problems in Advertising.* New York: McGraw-Hill, Inc., 1937.

——. *Advertising: Text and Cases.* Homewood, Ill.: Richard D. Irwin, Inc., 1949.

Borden, Neil H., and Marvin V. Marshall, *Advertising Management: Text and Cases:* Homewood, Ill.: Richard D. Irwin, Inc., 1959.

Burton, Jean. *Lydia Pinkham Is Her Name.* New York: Farrar, Strauss & Company, 1949.

Frankel, Lester R., in Russell H. Colley (ed.), *Evaluating Advertising Effectiveness, Volume VII.* New York: Association of National Advertisers, 1959.

Ferber, R., and P. J. Verdoorn, *Research Methods in Economics and Business.* New York: The Macmillan Company, 1962.

Howard, John A. *Marketing Management.* Homewood, Ill.: Richard D. Irwin, Inc., 1957.

Johnston, J. *Econometric Methods.* New York: McGraw-Hill, Inc., 1963.

Klapper, Joseph T. *The Effects of Mass Communications.* New York: The Free Press of Glencoe, Inc., 1960.

Klein, Lawrence R. *A Textbook of Econometrics.* New York: Harper & Row, Publishers, 1953.

Koyck, L. M. *Distributed Lags and Investment Analysis.* Amsterdam: North–Holland Publishing Co., 1954.

Nerlove, Marc. *Distributed Lags and Demand Analysis for Agricultural and Other Commodities.* U. S. Department of Agriculture Handbook No. 141. Washington, D.C.: Government Printing Office, June, 1959.

Pinkham, Charles. *Advertising, Volume I.* Lynn, Mass.: Lydia E. Pinkham Medicine Company, 1953.

Theil, H. *Economic Forecasts and Policy.* Second edition revised. Amsterdam: North–Holland Publishing Co., 1961.

Wolfe, H. D., G. K. Brown and G. C. Thompson, *Measuring Advertising Results.* New York: National Industrial Conference Board, 1962 (Business Policy Study No. 102).

Articles

Alt, F. L. "Distributed Lags," *Econometrica,* **X** (April, 1942), 113–28.

Cox, Donald F. "Clues for Advertising Strategists," *Harvard Business Review,* **XXXIX**, November-December, 1961. Reference is to reprint with unnumbered pages.

Fisher, Irving. "Note on a Short-Cut Method for Calculating Distributed Lags," *Bulletin de l'Institut International de la Statistique,* **XXIX** (1937), 323–27.

Hollander, Sidney. "A Rationale for Advertising Expenditures," *Harvard Business Review,* **XXVII** (January, 1949), 79–87.

Jastram, Roy W. "A Treatment of Distributed Lags in the Theory of Advertising Expenditure," *Journal of Marketing,* **XX** (July, 1955), 36–46.

Mendelsohn, Harold. "Measuring the Process of Communications Effect," *Public Opinion Quarterly,* **XXVI** (Fall, 1962), 411–16.

Mundlak, Yair. "Aggregation Over Time in Distributed Lag Models," *International Economic Review,* **II** (May, 1961), 154–63.

Nerlove, Marc. "Estimates of Elasticities of Supply of Selected Agricultural Commodities," *Journal of Farm Economics,* **XXXVIII** (May, 1956), 496–509.

Nerlove, Marc and Kenneth J. Arrow, "Optimal Advertising Policy under Dynamic Conditions," *Economica,* **XXXIX** (May, 1962), 129–42.

Nerlove, Marc and Frederick V. Waugh, "Advertising Without Supply Control: Some Implications of a Study of the Advertising of Oranges," *Journal of Farm Economics,* **XLIII** (October, 1961), 813–37.

Roberts, Harry V. "The Measurement of Advertising Results," *Journal of Business,* **XX** (July, 1947), 131–45.

Strohl, Lee. "Ladies of Lynn—Emphasis on One," *Surgery, Gynecology and Obstetrics,* (December, 1957), 755–69.

Telser, Lester G. "Advertising and Cigarettes," *Journal of Political Economy,* **LXX** (October, 1962), 471–99.

Theil, H. and A. L. Nagar, "Testing the Independence of Regression Disturbances," *Journal of the American Statistical Association,* **LVI** (December, 1961), 793–807.

Vidale, M. L. and H. B. Wolfe, "An Operations-Research Study of Sales Response to Advertising," *Operations Research,* **V** (June, 1957), 370–81.

Other Sources

Lydia E. Pinkham Medicine Company. Personal interviews and correspondence with the president and vice-president in charge of sales. Access to Company's sales and advertising records provided the source of the primary data for this dissertation.

Tull, Donald S. "An Examination of the Hypothesis that Advertising Has a Lagged Effect on Sales." Unpublished Ph.D. dissertation, University of Chicago, 1956.

U. S. Bureau of the Census. *Historical Statistics of the United States, Colonial Times to 1957.* Washington, 1960.